DUNCAN BOWIE

D1642886

RADICAL SOLUTIONS
TO THE HOUSING
SUPPLY CRISIS

POLICY PRESS SHORTS POLICY & PRACTICE

First published in Great Britain in 2017 by

Policy Press
University of Bristol
1-9 Old Park Hill
Bristol
BS2 8BB
UK
+44 (0)117 954 5940
pp-info@bristol.ac.uk
www.policypress.co.uk

North America office:
Policy Press
c/o The University of Chicago Press
1427 East 60th Street
Chicago, IL 60637, USA
t: +1 773 702 7700
f: +1 773 702 9756
sales@press.uchicago.edu
www.press.uchicago.edu

© Policy Press 2017

British Library Cataloguing in Publication Data
A catalogue record for this book is available from the British Library.

Library of Congress Cataloging-in-Publication Data
A catalog record for this book has been requested.

ISBN 978-1-4473-2849-0 (paperback)
ISBN 978-1-4473-3668-6 (ePub)
ISBN 978-1-4473-3667-9 (Mobi)
ISBN 978-1-4473-3666-2 (ePdf)

Cover design by Policy Press
Front cover: image kindly supplied by istock
Printed and bound in Great Britain by CMP, Poole
Policy Press uses environmentally responsible print partners

Contents

List of tables and figures   iv

Acknowledgements   v

Introduction   1

Section One: The context   5

1   Conservative government policy and the Housing and Planning Act 2016   7

2   Critiques of the current direction of government policy   25

3   The failure of governments since 1979 and the ideological continuities   51

Section Two: The crisis of housing supply   61

4   The housing deficit   63

5   Affordable by whom?   85

6   The wrong kind of homes   93

7   The inefficient use of the existing stock   99

8   The failure of the English planning system   105

Section Three: There is an alternative   119

9   A radical programme for reform   121

Conclusion: The four key issues   167

References   169

Index   177

List of tables and figures

List of tables

1.1	Housing capital investment in England since 2008	15
6.1	Density of new development in dwellings per hectare	94
7.1	Overcrowded and under-occupying households	101

List of figures

4.1	Developers' landbanks	66
5.1	The dynamic of affordability and tenure	89
5.2	Generational affordability	90
5.3	Young adults living with parents	91
5.4	Multi-family households	91
6.1	Location of development by tenure	97
7.1	Overcrowded households (dwellings with more than one person per habitable room)	101

Acknowledgements

Most of this book is derived from the work of the Highbury Group on Housing Delivery, the research and policy development academic/ practitioner network I have convened since 2008. While the drafting of the book is my own, I would like to thank the 60 or more colleagues who have contributed to the group's work over the last eight years. I would especially like to thank those group members who, within a very tight timescale at the end of the summer, were able to comment on the draft: Roger Jarman, Tony Manzi, Julia Atkins, Michael Edwards, Bob Colenutt, Deborah Garvie, Steve Hilditch and Peter Redman. The views expressed in the book are, however, my own, and I am aware that not all group members will agree with me on every point. Any errors are my own responsibility. I would also like to thank my immediate family, Jackie, Jenny and Chris, for their tolerance over the rather hectic few weeks in which this book was written, as well as the University of Westminster for hosting the Highbury Group's meetings over the last few years. My thanks also to Emily Watt and Laura Vickers at Policy Press. I recognise that there is a risk with any book of this kind that between writing and publication, housing policy may change, especially with a new set of ministers, and the book may have to be updated fairly quickly. I trust, however, that the basic principles for a new housing supply policy will stand for some time. If the government implements the recommended programme, there will be no need for a second edition.

INTRODUCTION

The premise of this book is that there is now a deep crisis in housing supply in many parts of England and that the policy proposals promoted by the government and many commentators are either just tinkering with the problem or will actually exacerbate the situation. We have not learnt the lessons of the 2008 credit crunch and, in fact, we have had a housing deficit whether the country has been in boom or bust. This book contends that we have failed to understand the fundamental deficiencies of the current system and that it is only by radical policy changes that the challenge can be met. It is time to throw off long-held ideological assumptions as to ideal forms of tenure and the relationship of state to market. In the last couple of years, as housing has moved up the political agenda, there has been a plethora of policy reports from think tanks and lobby groups proposing reform to existing housing and planning policy. However, in the view of this author, many of these proposals, if implemented, would have a relatively marginal impact. While there is widespread opposition to the government's recent legislation both within Parliament and from both professional and campaigning groups, there is less certainty as to what the alternative is and how we would get there. At the time of writing in September 2016, both the government and other interested parties are considering measures to intervene in housing delivery in the light of the downturn generated by the European Union (EU) referendum. This book argues that there is a systemic problem that cannot be corrected by short-term measures and that more radical solutions are necessary if the housing market is to be stabilised and the delivery of new homes increased.

I should note the limitations of this short book. First, it is about England. Wales, Scotland and Northern Ireland have their own housing policies as housing is a devolved function. They also have their own national spatial plans, something that England lacks.

The first section of the book sets out the context for the current housing supply crisis. The first chapter summarises the policies of the new Conservative government, focusing on the Housing and Planning Act 2016. The second chapter reviews academic critiques of the current policy direction of the government, while Chapter Three presents a summary analysis of the failures of successive governments since 1979 and reviews the ideological continuities.

The second section examines a number of key policy areas. Chapter Four discusses the overall housing supply deficit. Chapter Five focuses on the shortage of affordable housing for lower- and middle-income households. Chapter Six discusses the type and quality of the new homes being built. Chapter Seven considers the use of the existing housing stock. Chapter Eight explores the failures of the current planning system. The final section of the book sets out a reform programme, including the principles on which policies on housing supply should be based, before concluding with a package of specific policy reforms, covering investment policy, planning and land policy and taxation.

The book is about new housing supply. While there is consideration of how to make more effective use of the existing stock of housing in Chapter Seven, the book does not set out policies for the management of council and housing association homes, nor does it set out a reform package for the private rented sector or examine welfare policy and the operation of the housing benefit system. There is an academic literature and a plethora of policy reports on all of these issues, which I would not seek to duplicate. It should, however, be recognised that changes in the housing benefit system impact on housing supply and changes in housing supply in terms of both volume and affordability also have impacts on the overall housing benefit budget, as well as on a range of other government expenditure, for example, in relation to health, education and the criminal justice system. Given the space limitations, the factors impacting on the demand for housing are not considered in detail. There is no consideration of whether either population growth or in-migration or internal migration within the UK can be managed. It is recognised, however, that some of the taxation proposals are intended to suppress effective demand at the top end of the housing market.

I should also acknowledge that this book does have a focus on London and the South East. This is for three reasons – the first being that this is the part of England where the housing supply challenge is both most acute and most challenging to tackle. The second reason is that data sets for London tend to be more comprehensive than for the rest of the country, owing to the decision of central government to limit the publication of data at a regional level. In contrast, successive mayors of London have published relatively comprehensive data sets for the London region. The third reason is that for much of my professional as well as my academic career, I have focused on strategic planning and housing in London and the South East. I recognise that not all of the evidence and propositions in this book may be relevant to the challenges faced by other areas of England.

SECTION ONE
THE CONTEXT

1

CONSERVATIVE GOVERNMENT POLICY AND THE HOUSING AND PLANNING ACT 2016

Introduction

The Housing and Planning Act, which obtained Royal Assent on 12 May 2016, represents a fundamental redirection of housing and planning policy and can be seen as a fundamental shift from the post-war consensus. It is more significant than the Conservative government's Housing Act 1980, for as well as representing a further stage in the residualisation of the social housing sector, its planning provisions represent an abandonment of the basic principles of the Town and Country Planning Act 1947. The 2016 legislation, radical in its content and wide-ranging in its impacts, was rushed through Parliament in the final hours of the parliamentary session in April. It received little attention in the press and, despite the housing crisis having pushed the issue up the political agenda, little recognition in wider political circles, which were increasingly focused on the European Union referendum, the divisions in the Conservative Party, the continued inter-faction fighting in the Labour Party following the election of Jeremy Corbyn as leader and the mayoral contest in London.

Those who were either watching the legislation progress through the parliamentary process or actively trying to change it were conscious that it was a bad law. Leaving aside ideological debates as to the principles and objectives behinds the legislation, which will be discussed later, it was clear that the legislation was badly drafted. Hundreds of amendments were tabled to try and clarify the Bill's provisions, many by the government's own team. Moreover, the government added significant new clauses after the Bill had been through the scrutiny stage of the House of Commons Public Bill Committee. The government failed to publish any draft regulations and ministers were forced to make statements in the last few days of the parliamentary process as the Bill 'ping-ponged' between the Lords and Commons to try to provide reassurances that they knew what they were doing. There were no substantive impact assessments of the proposals and the government was unable to respond to questions as to how specific proposals within the legislation were actually to be delivered or how they were to be funded. While the Labour Party opposed the Bill in Parliament, the main opposition to the Bill, as well as more detailed scrutiny, came in the House of Lords, led by cross-benchers Lords Kerslake and Best, with relatively low-key and perhaps even half-hearted interventions by Labour peers. A number of Liberal peers pursued amendments on specific clauses, demonstrating the extent to which the pre-2015 Coalition had broken down. However, while the Lords appeared relatively progressive, carrying amendments against the government with majorities of about 100, in the Commons, the government had majorities of 100 or so as this was the first legislation to which the 'English votes for English laws' procedure applied and, as constitutional precedent required, the House of Commons overruled the Lords on all substantive amendments. This was despite the fact that many of the provisions were not set out in the Conservatives' general election manifesto, and nor were they all 'finance' provisions, which are traditionally regarded as the preserve of the House of Commons.

Given the significance of the provisions in the Act, which will be discussed later, it is perhaps surprising that many of the main interest groups were relatively quiescent. The Local Government Association, representing the country's statutory housing and planning authorities, under Conservative control, with their leader Lord Gary Porter in the Lords, did not raise substantive objections to the Bill and pursued, unsuccessfully, relatively minor changes. The Chartered Institute of Housing and the Royal Town Planning Institute, no doubt wishing to preserve their relationships with the government, again focused on seeking technical amendments rather than seeking to challenge the overall direction of the legislation. The Town and Country Planning Association pursued its traditional agenda of trying to encapsulate garden city principles and general sustainable development principles in the legislation. More vigorous opposition to the Bill came from Defend Council Housing, who established a 'Kill the Bill' campaign, with marches in London and other major cities and protest meetings within the parliamentary precincts – all to no avail. In post-mortems, many commentators are asking the question as to why it was so easy for the government to make such fundamental and negative changes to established housing and planning policy.

Some may question the view that this new legislation is so significant. It can be argued that the Act itself only represents a further stage in a direction of travel that has been clear since 1979, a direction that has been largely continuous through successive governments – Thatcher and Major, Blair and Brown, and Cameron's Coalition government up to 2015. There is some truth in this view and, to some extent, Labour's opposition to the Bill was constrained and somewhat embarrassed by the fact that some of the Bill's content, for example, in relation to 'better-off' council tenants paying market rents or reducing security of tenure for council tenants, drew on propositions put forward by Labour ministers in previous governments. The new Labour leadership had a different perspective, but although clearer in their opposition to the Conservative agenda, they were less clear on their own alternative beyond some broad objectives and were lacking in any confidence about how to deliver them. Later in this short book, I will set out the principles of an alternative housing and planning policy, as well as some of the potential mechanisms for delivering this alternative.

In this introductory chapter, however, it is necessary to set out the provisions of the new Act and to relate it to other policy and funding changes introduced by the Conservative government and its immediate predecessor, the Conservative-led Coalition. This Act, enacted in May 2016, includes a number of provisions that are likely to have significant impacts on the provision of affordable housing in England, with its negative impacts being most significant in London and other areas where the shortage of affordable homes is most acute.

The provisions of the Housing and Planning Act include:

- The extension of the 'Right to Buy' to housing associations on a 'voluntary basis' funded by the disposal by councils of 'higher-value properties' when they become vacant. The government will raise a levy on councils based on assumptions about value and vacancy rates, irrespective of whether or not properties have actually been sold. However, the government has not yet defined the high-value thresholds either at a regional or local level. The government has stated that every home sold should be replaced, with a 2:1 replacement target in London. However, there is no requirement that the replacement should be on a 'like-for-like' basis either in terms of tenure, affordability, dwelling type or location. The government resisted amendments that would have allowed local authorities to use sales receipts to provide replacement social rented homes.

- The government has introduced a new 'starter homes' programme. Homes on sale at up to £450,000 in London and £250,000 outside London will be deemed to be affordable in terms of planning policy and exempt from planning obligations and the Community Infrastructure Levy (the optional local authority development tax to provide funding for transport and social infrastructure). This is on the basis that such homes will be at a discount of 20% on market value. The purchaser will only have to repay this discount if they resell the property within five years of purchase. Purchasers must be under 40 (though can have older partners) and may be subject to nationality requirements. As yet, the government has not clarified whether thresholds will be varied locally or related to the size of the home. At present, the threshold does not distinguish between studio flats and large detached houses. Councils will be required to use 20% of their residential development capacity to provide 'starter homes' irrespective of whether or not their strategic housing market assessment demonstrates this level of effective demand. The government resisted amendments that would have limited the obligation to provide starter homes to areas where effective demand was demonstrated. The Minister has the power to amend local plan policies where they are considered to be obstructing the delivery of the starter homes target.

- Under provisions known somewhat inappropriately as 'pay to stay', council tenants on incomes of over £40,000 a year in London (£31,000 elsewhere) will be required to pay up to market rents. The government has proposed that increases are phased via a 15% taper, with caps related to household income. Tenants in receipt of housing benefit and universal credit will be exempt.

- Under provisions for 'fixed-term tenancies', new council tenants will only be entitled to a tenancy between two and five years. The Localism Act 2011 had allowed councils to introduce minimum two-year tenancies but few had chosen to do so. It is unclear whether a range of vulnerable groups, including tenants transferring to new tenancies, can be exempted from this provision and issued with secure tenancies.

- The Minister has a new power to set aside planning obligations agreed between councils and developers.

- Ministers are introducing a system of alternative providers who can compete to provide local authority planning services, with differential standards and fee rates.

- A new form of planning consent was introduced – 'permission in principle' – by which a landowner, investor or developer can be granted planning permission for housing with key policy issues such as built form, mix, tenure, affordability and amenities to be resolved at a later 'technical' stage.

Most of the debate on the Bill, both within Parliament and outside it, focused on the housing provisions of the Bill. These are an extension of the attack by successive governments on social housing, and reflect the abandonment of the post-war consensus that the government had a responsibility to provide homes for those unable to access the private market. The planning provisions, which attracted less attention, were equally significant. The requirement on local councils to provide for 'starter homes', with a fixed target for each area irrespective of any assessment of effective demand, moves away from the concept of a plan-based system under which each plan is required to be based on evidence, an approach based on the Town and Country Planning Act 1947, which itself reflected the pre-First World War mantra of 'survey before plan' advocated by Patrick Geddes. One of the purposes of this book is to relate the current policy direction of the government to the fundamental principles of housing and planning policy established by progressive governments in the years after the Second World War, principles that are now largely forgotten by ministers and their advisors.

Despite the current government's 'localist' rhetoric, the new Act has given the secretary of state new powers to require a local council to amend its plan, as well as powers to override planning obligation agreements between councils and developers. A council that had agreed a development on the basis that the developer would ensure compliance with the council's planning policy objectives or mitigate the scheme's negative impacts could find these requirements overridden in order to protect the viability or profitability of the developer. The relationship between the statutory planning authority and the private developer was fundamentally changed – the local authority duty was no longer to protect the public interest, but to enable private investment and asset appreciation. This represents an abandonment of the fundamental principles of the post-war consensus established in the Town and Country Planning Act 1947. This book sets out the reasons why these principles remain important. Chapter Two will discuss how we have reached this sorry state of affairs.

However, the Housing and Planning Act 2016 was only one phase of a policy shift initiated when the Coalition government was elected in

May 2010. That government terminated the government programme of funding social rented housing through investment grants, a programmed managed since 1974 initially by the Housing Corporation and from 2008 by the Homes and Communities Agency. While successive governments had increased the share of the programme that supported homeownership initiatives, notably, the shared ownership programme, the Coalition government, with Eric Pickles as Secretary of State for Communities and George Osborne as Chancellor of the Exchequer, switched the social rent investment programme to a new rented housing programme designated as 'affordable rent' on the basis that with rents up to 80% of market rates, the level of government grant per home could be substantially reduced. The average grant per new home fell from £51,178 during 2008/09–2010/11 to £21,920 during 2011/12–2014/15. The overall national investment programme was cut from £2.97 billion a year in the last years of the New Labour government to £0.45 billion a year in the Coalition government's 2011/12–2014/5 programme (CIH, 2016). Ministers had the objective of increasing the output of sub-market housing but were perhaps less concerned as to who could actually afford the homes built.

The Localism Act 2011, which will be discussed further later, gave local authorities considerable flexibility in terms of homelessness duties, lettings policies and tenancy conditions, removing the notion of open access to and national standard conditions of occupation of council homes and removing tenure choice for homeless households. In response to concerns as to the costs to the exchequer of increasing housing benefit, which reflected increasing rents in the private rented, local authority and housing association sectors, the government introduced a series of limits to housing benefits per household: the introduction of housing allowance caps for private renters; the extension to social housing of the limit on housing benefit payment to households in social housing considered to have more bedrooms than they needed, which the government referred to as the removal of the 'spare room subsidy' but that was more popularly known as the 'bedroom tax' (Cowan and Marsh, 2016); the extension of the shared accommodation rate applying to the under 25s to the under

35s; and the introduction of an overall welfare benefit cap for all households, at £26,000 a year for London families and £20,000 a year for families in the rest of England, which is due to be reduced still further. The government also increased the level of discount for council tenants seeking to exercise the 'Right to Buy' in an attempt to further increase the number of homeowners and further reduce the stock of social housing.

The Coalition government also introduced significant changes to the planning system. Their first move was to abolish the regional planning system. The regional assemblies and regional development agencies were shut down and the eight regional plans for English regions outside London were abolished, even though some of the plans had only been adopted a few months earlier. The government abandoned the previous government's sustainable communities plan and withdrew support for the growth areas, growth points and eco-towns, which had received government revenue support and prioritisation for capital investment. In line with its 'localist' agenda, the government withdrew all regional targets, which were seen as bureaucratic impositions, and took the view that residential growth should only take place if it was locally initiated and supported by local communities, an approach reinforced by the provisions for neighbourhood planning introduced in the Localism Act 2011. The Coalition government also amended the definition of affordable housing to include all forms of sub-market provision, including the new 'affordable rent' programme, with local authorities and the mayor of London required to amend any adopted planning policies that set separate targets for new lower-rented housing, whether provided by local authorities, housing associations or other providers. A series of government statements, including the 'Planning for growth' statement in 2011 (DBIS/DCLG, 2011) and the *National planning policy framework* (NPPF) (DCLG, 2012) published in 2012, made it clear that the main focus of planning should be to support economic growth. The Prime Minister, David Cameron, was explicit in his view that planners were obstructing growth. The provisions of the Housing and Planning Act 2016 therefore need to be seen within this wider context.

Table 1.1: Housing capital investment in England since 2008

Affordable Housing Programme 2008/9–2010/11 (out-turn)	£8.9 billion	£2.97b pa
Affordable Housing Programme 2011/12–2014/15 (out-turn)	£1.8 billion	£0.45b pa
Affordable Housing Programme 2015/16–2017/18 (budget)	£2.9 billion	£0.96b pa
Forecast spend 2015/16–2017/18	£1.8 billion	£0.60b pa
Average grant per dwelling (England)		
2008/9–2010/11	£51,178	
2011/12–2014/15	£21,920	
2015/16–2017/18	£17,454	

Source: CIH (2016)

Starter homes

The most prominent proposal within the new provisions was the starter homes initiative. A primary concern is that the initiative will do more to inflate house prices than to increase supply and will therefore worsen rather than mitigate the current crisis of housing affordability (SHELTER, 2015; LGA, 2016). The proposal to consider homes at up to £450,000 in London and £250,000 in the rest of England as affordable in terms of planning policy, and to remove the obligations of any such developments to contribute towards the provision of community benefits (including genuinely affordable homes) through section 106 agreements and contributions to infrastructure through the Community Infrastructure Levy, is not based on any analysis of households' ability to afford such homes. Moreover, it will reduce the ability of local authorities to implement adopted plan policies, which seek to provide a wider range of housing needs, including accommodation at social and sub-market rents and shared ownership provision, in relation to their assessment of housing requirements through strategic housing market assessments in accordance with the pre-existing requirements in the NPPF and national planning policy guidance. The revised national definition of affordable housing invalidates policies in existing development plans, including the London Plan, which had been adopted following public consultation, Examinations in Public and inspectors' reports, and which had demonstrated compliance with the pre-existing NPPF as well as with other components of the soundness test applied by planning inspectors.

The legislation also removed the requirement that affordable homes should be affordable in perpetuity. The starter homes initiative is predicated on a direct or indirect subsidy to purchasers of up to 20% relative to market value, with the purchaser granted this value after five years. This is, in effect, a subsidy from public resources (whether in terms of direct grant or exemption from planning obligations and the Community Infrastructure Levy) to those households who can afford to buy homes at up to £450,000 in London and £250,000 in the rest of England, households whose incomes will generally be significantly above the average incomes of households in their respective areas.

The government's intention to issue specific starter homes targets for individual local authorities has the risk of overriding local planning authorities' (LPAs') own assessments of, and policies for the provision of, different types of housing in terms of tenure and affordability. The government did not provide any evidence for its 200,000 target in relation to any assessment of national housing requirements or national housing development capacity. The government has also insisted that the 20% of total capacity target should apply to each local authority irrespective of any evidence of requirements at regional or local level or any targets in existing adopted plan policies. This is further complicated by the fact that existing strategic housing market assessments do not generally assess the effective demand for homes at 80% of market value, as assessments will generally relate to effective demand for market-value homes and for other pre-existing products such as social rent, shared ownership and, in some cases, forms of sub-market rent, including in recent assessments the effective demand for housing at up to 80% market rent in accordance with the government's 'affordable rent' product.

The government has also stated that to qualify for homes provided under the starter homes initiative, the purchaser will need to be under 40, though apparently purchasers can have partners over 40 and ex-servicepersons are exempted from this requirement. As the government's own equalities statement itself recognised, such a policy discriminates against older households and creates difficulties for providers of retirement housing, where the minimum age is typically specified as 60. The government has also focused on starter homes only being available for UK citizens, though it is unclear how this requirement is to be policed and also ignores the fact that many prospective marginal homeowners who are active contributors to the UK economy and to essential public services such as health or education may not be UK citizens. This proposal therefore contrasts with the government objective that housing policy should support national economic growth. It is, however, unlikely in the post-Brexit era that this condition will be relaxed as the focus is increasingly on British homes for British people.

Right to Buy

The extension of the Right to Buy to housing association tenants leads to a reduction in the supply of social housing available at relatively low rents that are affordable by households on lower incomes, including working households, without overreliance on housing benefit support. The government's argument that the initiative will generate an increase in the supply of affordable homes has no basis in any evidence provided by the government and is not supported by the experience of the Right to Buy scheme for council tenants, where actual practice has demonstrated a significant underperformance in relation to the government's objective of 1:1 replacement.

As yet, ministers have not specified the form of replacement required, with the implication that it is for the housing association concerned to decide whether a sold dwelling is replaced by a new dwelling in the same area, of the same size and type, and at the same rent. If the replacement can be of a different tenure (eg shared ownership), at a higher rent (up to 80% market rent), with a smaller bedroom size or smaller space standard, or in a different location – for example, one where effective demand is lower or build and land costs are lower – then it is likely that, in qualitative terms if not in quantitative terms, there will be a reduction in the supply of affordable homes. Homes needed in higher-demand areas such as London will be replaced by new homes in lower-demand areas. It is also questionable whether the provisions in relation to replacement, so far as they are known, allow an association to continue to comply with its charitable objectives. The government failed to publish a full impact assessment in relation to the Act's provisions and to demonstrate that, when combined with other measures proposed in the Bill, including the disposal of high-value local authority properties and the non-renewal of five-year local authority tenancies, they would not have a negative impact on the financial and social circumstances of lower-income households or on the housing and welfare benefit budgets. The most detailed impact assessment yet undertaken, published by the Joseph Rowntree Foundation, concluded that there will be a significant negative impact in relation to both these factors (JRF, 2016).

Forced sale of vacant higher-value council homes

The requirement imposed on local authorities to dispose of higher-value residential assets or to pay a levy to central government in relation to the value of such assets is clearly contrary to the general principle that local authorities should be responsible for the management of their assets in relation to their statutory duties. The provisions could lead to a significant loss of affordable housing in higher-value areas such as central London. They will also act as a disincentive to local authorities seeking to invest in new housing provision through direct development as most new development would be covered by disposal requirements once the first tenant vacated the property. Moreover, in reducing the amount of social housing available for letting, the proposals will increase the dependence of lower-income households on private rented housing, which not only reduces their security and quality of life, but also significantly increases housing benefit costs. There is a possibility that lower-income households, including working households, will be forced to move away from higher-value areas. This would lead to further spatial social polarisation, contrary to objectives for having mixed communities, and will increase demands on the public transport system as dispersed residents will need to travel further to work. Given the cost of public transport, this may not be affordable by workers on lower incomes.

The provisions also have serious implications for local authorities, who will not be able to make most effective use of their assets and, in fact, will not be able to retain receipts from enforced disposals as the levy will be used by the government to compensate housing associations for the loss of assets through the application of 'Right to Buy' discounts. The proposals for a mandatory extraction of value from public sector assets in order to compensate housing associations for the loss of their assets, which will now be on the basis of a voluntary decision by each registered provider rather than as a statutory requirement, has neither a logical basis nor, for that matter, any precedent. It is, in effect, an abuse of public assets funded by revenue from taxpayers for government to impose a statutory transfer of public assets to housing associations that are, in effect, independent bodies. The government has so far failed to demonstrate any public benefit from this proposal, the main justification being that the proposal contributes to its objective of increasing homeownership.

Pay to stay

The government has also failed to provide adequate evidence to support the provision that council tenants on above-average incomes should pay market rents. While the provisions only apply on a statutory basis to council tenancies, housing associations were also encouraged to adopt a similar approach, though it is for individual housing associations to determine whether or not they adopt a similar approach. The government's original intention was that households above the income threshold should immediately pay higher rents. After it was pointed out that this could mean a trebling of rents for some households in council homes in areas where market rents were very high, the government agreed to phase in higher rents via a 15% taper, related to household income above the relevant threshold. The government's proposals seem to be predicated on the false assumption that all council tenants are subsidised. However, at a national level, the aggregate of council housing revenue accounts is in surplus, so that there is, in fact, no overall subsidy towards the costs of providing council homes, other than through benefit payments to tenants. To charge some tenants market-level rents would therefore to be to charge them rents in excess of the services that they are receiving. In other words, 'higher-income' tenants will be subsidising not just other tenants, but the provision of council services as a whole. The policy fundamentally changes the notion of rents based on the nature of the home and service supplied to rents based on the tenant's ability to pay. This could be seen as penalising tenants who have sought to maximise their earnings and thereby creating a disincentive to do so.

The proposals lead to the further residualisation of council housing in that they would lead to the further concentration of the lowest-income households within the cheapest council housing as the housing with lowest rents is generally of poor quality and/or in a less desirable location. This is contrary to the government objective of maintaining mixed communities and ensuring the economic sustainability of neighbourhoods in which council housing is still the predominant tenure. Moreover, the income thresholds proposed (£40,000 in London and £31,000 in the rest of England) do not appear to relate to whether or not appropriate alternative accommodation that is affordable to the household is actually available in the local area.

Furthermore, the new policy introduces an intrusive landlord–tenant relationship, whereby tenants are required to regularly disclose their income details or face the prospect of maximum rent increases. In order to establish which minority of tenants are caught by the policy, landlords will be required to collect income details from every single tenant, creating huge bureaucracy and the risk of the mischarging of rent leading to repossession for notional arrears.

Flexible tenancies

The government's justification for the proposal to limit the maximum tenancy of local authority tenants to five years was that local authorities had not generally used the powers in the Localism Act 2011 to grant new tenancies of between two and five years. This rather discounts the possibility that local authorities of varying political control may have decided not to use this power because they did not see the benefit of doing so. It does seem contrary to the basic principle that local authorities know how to best utilise their assets in relation to their statutory duties and assessment of local needs for the government to then impose a requirement that not only reduces tenants' rights and security, but also forces local authorities to operate a bureaucratic procedure that they themselves do not consider to be necessary. The government has been unclear on whether it is going to specify any criteria on the basis of which a local authority could decide not to renew a tenancy at the end of a five-year period, or on the properties or types of tenants that could be exempt from the requirement, nor has the government specified whether a tenant could have the right of appeal against non-renewal. Moreover, the interaction with Right to Buy is unclear in relation to whether a tenant loses their Right to Buy entitlement, which they can exercise after a three-year tenancy, once notification of non-renewal has been issued, whether or not they have already given the council notice of their wish to exercise that right.

The provisions will have a serious negative impact on lower-income households, including vulnerable households, for whom their security of tenure (which is, after all, conditional on not breaching tenancy conditions) may be the most stable component of their lives given the insecurity of employment and the impact of other external circumstances.

'In principle' planning consent

One of the key features of the planning reforms within the Housing and Planning Act was the introduction of an 'in principle' planning consent. This is linked to a new power for the secretary of state to issue a local development order for a site or group of sites. While ministers have implied that the use of these powers will be limited to either small sites or sites on brownfield site registers, the clauses in the Act do not include any such limitation. The notion of separating an 'in principle' consent for housing development from a 'technical' consent process is fundamentally flawed. Ministers struggled to explain why such a new procedure was required given that LPAs already have the power to grant outline consent for schemes. In practice, many LPAs require a full planning application in order to ensure that the proposed development complies with published planning policy. As yet, the government has not issued any clarification as to what matters could be considered by the LPA through the technical consent process. In the Public Bill Committee scrutinising the Bill, the minister commented 'that matters such as affordable housing contribution and community infrastructure provision will be agreed and negotiated at the later technical details stage, in line with local and national policy' (Lewis, 2015).

However, these matters are not technical matters, but may, in some cases, be fundamental to an LPA's consideration of whether the site is or is not suitable for housing development, together with matters such as the density and built form of development, the bedroom size mix of development, quality standards, or flood risk mitigation. An LPA decision in relation to a housing development proposal is not solely whether a site is suitable 'in principle' for a housing development, but whether the proposed development contributes to meeting the requirements assessed in the strategic housing market assessment, in accordance with national policy, as set out in the NPPF and the national planning policy guidance.

The Act included provisions relating to speeding up the process of compulsory purchase. However, it fails to deal with the key issue of land assembly for the development of affordable housing, that is, the price paid for land in relation to the existing land value. For housing of any tenure to be available at a price or rent affordable by households on middle or lower incomes, it is essential that land cost is minimised and that the landowner does not benefit unduly from the fact that land is allocated for residential development in an adopted statutory plan or from the granting of planning consent for a residential or residential-led development. We agree with the minister's view that land price should reflect existing planning policy requirements. Any relaxation of policies in relation to density, built form and affordable housing requirements, however, inflates land costs. As will be discussed further later, the Act could have set the basis for the acquisition of land for development, including compulsory purchase by public bodies, at existing use value plus a limited fixed premium to be determined by regulations. This premium could be a fixed proportionate premium relating to the pre-existing land use and the value of that use.

Weakening of local authority planning

The Act included two further significant planning measures. The first is a provision for the secretary of state to override any planning agreement that a developer had entered into with the planning authority. The second is a provision for alternative providers to compete with local authorities in the provision of statutory planning services. Both these proposals were introduced into the Bill after it had been subject to scrutiny in the Bill Committee in the House of Commons. Both these proposals, disguised as mechanisms for speeding up the delivery of new homes, are predicated on giving the developer and private planning consultants greater power in relationship to the local authority, further increasing the previous market sector bias in the planning system.

The overall impact of the 2016 Act

Overall, the Act presented a further attack on social housing in terms of both reducing existing social housing supply and constraining the provision of further social housing. It also represented an attack on social housing tenants – forcing many thousands of existing tenants to pay higher rents while reducing the security of new tenants. The Act represents a further centralisation of housing and planning decision-making at a time when local authorities are dealing with acute resource constraints and having to address growing demand for housing and homelessness assistance to meet their statutory duties. The Act also reduces a local authority's ability to use its planning powers to ensure the provision of the range of homes required in its area and for the first time introduced a requirement for a local authority to prioritise provision of one specific housing product – the starter home – irrespective of its own assessment of the relative needs for different types of housing. Chapter Two will discuss some critiques of the current direction of government policy while Chapter Three will briefly examine some of the historical background to this policy position.

2

CRITIQUES OF THE CURRENT DIRECTION OF GOVERNMENT POLICY

For the last two decades, there has been a large degree of consensus between the Conservative and Labour Parties on the appropriate government approach to housing policy and specifically to intervention in the housing market and the supply of new homes. This consensus is now being challenged. While Chapter Three will seek to trace some of the policy developments since the early 1980s, this chapter is intended to review the debates on housing policy within the last decade, focusing on the Labour Party and progressive engaged academics and practitioners in the period before and after the 2015 general election. In doing so, the author is not intending to focus on academic critiques of the current consensus or the wider debates on the impact of neoliberalism on urban development, including the work of Harvey (1989, 2006, 2007) and Berry (2014), among others. It is necessary, however, to acknowledge that three fundamental critiques exist. The first is the neoliberal critique from academics such as Paul Cheshire (Cheshire et al, 2014) and Alun Evans (Evans and Hartwich, 2005), a critique shared by many policy advocates working within the Policy Exchange think tank, including Alex Morton, policy advisor to the prime minister until spring 2016, and Nick Boles, Planning Minister in the 2010–15 administration. This critique argues that the main constraint on housing delivery and therefore affordability is the bureaucratic and constraining planning system, which excludes a significant proportion of land, notably, the green belt, from development, and therefore that a liberalisation of planning would have a positive outcome.

A second perspective is that of Danny Dorling (2014), who argues that there is no actual housing supply crisis in England, but that there is a problem of distribution, that is, that the housing stock needs to be more fairly distributed. There is a third critique, that of Costas Lapavitsas (2013), which argues that the housing crisis is primarily the product of the financialisation of capital – that capital is now focused on investment rather than production. The view of the author is that each of these critiques have considerable validity but that the crisis we face is a product of a wide range of factors and that no single theory presents a satisfactory contextualisation. As argued later, the current situation arises from a combination of factors, including the ownership of land, the lack of public sector resources, the ownership of housing assets and the distribution of power between the public and private sector. The author therefore largely shares the analysis presented in the recent work of Edwards (2015), Cochrane et al (2015) and Hill (2015).

Some reference should also be made to the radical academic critique of housing and urban governance based on the concept of the 'right to the city', the notion that none should be denied access to housing and other urban services by reason of lack of wealth or income, class or ethnicity, or other characteristics that can lead to forms of exclusion or marginalisation. There is an extensive literature derived from the French sociologist and urbanist Henri Lefevre (1985, 1991), which has been picked up by a range of Marxist academics such as David Harvey (2008), Margit Meyer (2009), Neil Brenner (Brenner et al 2011) and the former United Nations (UN) housing commissioner Raquel Rolnik (2014), as well as more recently by Peter Marcuse and David Madden (2016) with regards to housing in New York. The slogan of 'right to the city' or, more specifically, 'right to a home' has been utilised by a range of political organisations and campaigning groups, not just in the UK, but internationally. Even the Labour Housing Group published a volume of essays entitled *Right to a home* in 1984 (Labour Housing Group, 1984). The difficulty with a slogan that is, in effect, a demand, however inspirational, is that while expressing understandable collective dissatisfaction with the role that housing inequity plays within governance and society as a whole, the slogan does not in itself generate a solution or even a transitional programme pending the abolition and/or collapse of the capitalist system as it does not establish how, after the revolution, equity of access to good-quality affordable housing will be provided or funded. As will be discussed later, redistribution of the existing housing stock, whether through legal or illegal methods, does not on its own mean that everybody can live where they want to. Even self-build has a cost. The parallel academic literature on the 'just city' (eg Fainstein, 2010; Soja, 2011), which can trace its origins to traditions of Christian communism (see Bowie, 2016a), has similar notions but, in effect, is a critique without a programme.

The perspective that there is a range of contributing factors produces the conclusion that no single policy intervention will in itself correct the current deficiencies, and the purpose of this book is both to demonstrate the inadequacy of the current policy and to present a range of options that, in combination, could provide a more appropriate response to the challenges faced. The aim is to present a package of interventions that both challenge the current direction of government policy and generate a fundamental policy shift. However, it is first necessary to briefly review how the current context is different from those previous periods in which housing supply outcomes were more positive.

The period after the end of the Second World War witnessed a consensus that the state at both national and local level had a key role in ensuring the provision of homes for the population as a whole. An initial emergency housing programme of prefabricated homes was undertaken, followed by a national programme of investment in new council housing. The Town and Country Planning Act 1947 introduced a comprehensive system of local authority-led planning, with all development controlled by local planning authorities and a system for land value appreciation from development being used for public policy purposes. The government also initiated a national programme of state-funded major new settlements – new towns – which contrasted with the private philanthropic settlements of the earlier garden cities era. While the later Conservative government first abolished the land value capture system and also boosted private house-building, the national consensus that the state had a responsibility to plan, fund and own housing for households who could not afford market provision held throughout the 1950s, 1960s and early 1970s (Merrett, 1979; Malpass, 2003; Bowie, 2012b). The mid-1960s saw a brief but failed attempt to establish a system of national state planning with George Brown's short-lived national plan, but national support for public housing remained and it was only with the International Monetary Fund (IMF) intervention and the crisis of the Callaghan government, with Denis Healey as chancellor, in the late 1970s that we witnessed a significant withdrawal of the state from public sector investment. The Thatcher government elected in 1979 pursued an agenda of state withdrawal from welfare provision and of privatisation, pursuing a neoliberalist economic agenda. Councils were forced to sell council homes to tenants under the Housing Act 1980, while from 1984, the role of providing new homes for lower-income households was shifted from local councils to housing associations – funded and regulated by the state through the Housing Corporation but notionally independent. Local authorities were also encouraged and, in fact, incentivised to transfer their housing stock to housing associations and to transfer the management of their homes to housing associations or private management companies.

The Labour governments of 1997–2010 did little to resist this neoliberal agenda, and the approach of the Thatcher and Major governments was continued by the Blair government that came to power in 1997. The Blair government continued the move to reliance on the private sector for housing provision. It continued to promote the transfer of council housing to private ownership through the continuation of the Right To Buy, but also made funding of the improvement of council estates dependent on local authorities surrendering control of the management of its housing, with grant funding for the decent homes programme being conditional on the transfer of housing management to arm's-length management organisations (ALMOs). The government-sponsored Housing Corporation funding system for new-build moved from the initial regime that funded 100% of capital costs, to a mixed funding regime that used private finance repayable from rent income together with levels of grant ranging from 30% to 70% of capital costs, to a programme that relied on competitive bids from providers – not just housing associations, but private developers, who could become eligible for grants as 'registered providers'. An increasing proportion of the programme – up to 40% of capital investment – was used to support homeownership initiatives such as shared ownership and sub-market rented initiatives such as the key workers programme, in contrast with the more traditional housing association product of social rented homes. With the reduction of the level of capital grant per new housing association home, housing associations became increasingly dependent on cross-subsidy from private developments, often delivered through planning gain agreements negotiated by the local authority. As government funding for new social infrastructure was also constrained, local authorities became increasingly dependent on planning gain to support the essential infrastructure required for major new developments. The government also introduced a new target rent system, the intention of which was to raise council rents, which had previously been locally determined by local authorities, to be equivalent to the level of housing association rents, including introducing a component of the rent that related to property value, pushing up the level of council rents in higher-value areas such as central London.

In 2004, the Brown government commissioned the economist Kate Barker to review the causes of the undersupply of housing. The Barker review focused on the relationship between overall market housing supply and house price inflation, and did not reconsider the lack of government investment in housing and infrastructure as a key factor in undersupply, instead arguing that the planning system was at fault both in constraining land supply and in slowing down actual development through its 'bureaucratic' controls. Rather curiously given its focus on market supply, the review did not actually consider the availability of mortgage finance as a relevant factor. In practice, the house price boom of the mid-2000s had been fuelled by an unregulated supply of mortgage finance, with loans available to middle-income households without adequate security and at levels beyond the capacity of households to repay – known in retrospect as sub-prime lending – a practice common with elements of the US mortgage market, where much of the lending was by state-supported lenders.

The Brown government was to argue that the global financial crisis originated in the US. However, the extent of deregulation of the financial markets and the lack of controls over borrowing was a facet of the UK market as well as the US market. The Brown government intervened to bail out the UK banks and building societies that were at risk of default and, in doing so, contributed to saving the world economy or at least the Anglo-American financial system. The crisis had a dramatic impact on both the housing market and the housing development programme. It generated a mortgage famine, which meant that prospective homeowners could not raise the finance to buy as lenders required deposits of up to 25% of value. Property values fell by between 10% and 20%. Property transactions fell by 50%. Developers had to write off millions of pounds in land values, and the house-builders' development programme came to a standstill, some half-built schemes bring mothballed.

The government's intention was to reactivate the lending market and get the housing market back to normal. To rescue the development programme, the Brown government allocated extra resources to the Housing Corporation under the 'kickstart' programme to get development going again – in practice, this meant providing shared-ownership funding and some social rented funding for some stalled market-led schemes. However, the government failed to use its ownership of banks and house-builders to redirect finance into the house-building sector, or to ensure that schemes that were no longer viable were redesigned to provide homes to meet the changed market or include higher proportions of social rented and shared-ownership housing. Instead, the government advised local planning authorities to extend the timescale of developer consent in order to give time for the market to recover. They also put pressure on councils to reduce their requirements for affordable homes, and, in fact, the Coalition government elected in 2010 went so far as to introduce legislation in the Growth and Infrastructure Act 2013 to allow house-builders to seek government intervention to revise planning obligation agreements where, post-recession, the developer could show that they could no longer deliver the agreed affordable housing outputs, normally where the house-builder had overpaid for the land before the recession. The government took the view that the best way to stimulate was to deregulate planning and to incentivise house-builders.

Government approaches to housing since the early 1980s have been partly based on the perspective that the role of the state should be reduced as most public services can be provided by the private market but also reflect what is referred to as the 'austerity' agenda: that public expenditure should be retrenched and that the government, often presented as 'the country', cannot afford high levels of public investment. While the argument for the devolution of decision-making and a reduction in the role of the central state is often presented as a 'democratic' argument (which will be considered in a later chapter when the relationship of localism to planning is considered), the argument for state withdrawal is also presented in economic terms: that any public expenditure funded by taxation is a withdrawal of resources from a productive private economy and that it is in the broader public interest for public expenditure to be minimised – the fundamental position promoted by both left- and right-wing libertarian think tanks that taxation is inherently a bad thing. This argument, and the economic case for a minimum state, can be traced back to early 'liberal' moral and economic thinkers such as Locke, Hume and the early J.S. Mill (Blyth, 2015). The case for public investment funded out of taxation to support essential state functions, including housing, education, health and welfare support for households lacking the wealth or income to access the market, was presented by the New Liberals of the pre-First World War period. The focus on austerity government, most notably, in the post-2008 period, in other words, under the governments of Brown, Cameron and now Theresa May, accepts the view that government expenditure, and government tax take, has to be reduced in order to promote economic growth and that the maintenance of basic welfare state services, whether the National Health Service (NHS), education or housing provision, is secondary to economic growth supported by a deficit reduction agenda. This broad approach was accepted by the Labour Party in the post-2008 period, just as it was accepted by the Labour Party under the leadership of James Callaghan in the 1977–79 recession. Of course, this austerity/retrenchment approach to economic recession reflects a rejection of all the basic principles of Keynesian economics, but there is a much more fundamental point: that austerity politics is actually a matter of political choice, not of economic necessity. Just as it is a matter of political choice how a government spends its resources – for example, whether to prioritise its military capacity or its housing programme – it is also a matter of political choice how much and from what sources it raises revenue to fund government expenditure. A government can choose to increase or reduce rates of taxes on wealth and income for different types of households or corporate bodies, or for different forms of consumer expenditure. Any new administration that considers tax policy as fixed is inevitably limiting is policy choices in terms of levels of public expenditure, a key error made by the Labour government in 1997, and a key error in Labour Party policy in the run-up to both the 2010 and 2015 general elections. This notion of austerity governance is the key obstacle to solving the housing supply crisis in England. It is significant that while in both post-war periods, there was a recognition that government resources were limited and that the use of resources needed to be tightly managed, there was also a recognition that investment in reconstruction should not be constrained by concerns regarding deficit reduction, at least until the 'Geddes axe' of 1922 and the post-Second World War

Labour government's retrenchment in 1950–51. In previous periods of much more severe resource constraints – in other words, periods of genuine austerity – much greater government investment had been focused on housing supply that in the recent period of government-chosen 'austerity' in what is, after all, one of the wealthiest countries in the world – at least in terms of private wealth rather than in terms of public wealth (Bowie, 2012b).

The Conservative–Liberal Democrat Coalition government returned in May 2010 extended the deregulatory approach of the previous government. Its most radical approach was to terminate central government investment in new social rented housing. Not only was the investment budget inherited from the Labour government cut by about 70%, but the investment in social rent was switched to a new programme, misnamed as 'affordable rent', which was to support a programme of rented homes at much higher rents – up to 80% of market rent. In parts of England where market rents were high, such as London and the South East, this meant that rents for new housing association homes could be twice or three times as high as pre-existing housing association and council rents. The view of the new government was that this would produce more 'affordable' homes at significantly less cost to the public sector – in London, for example, capital grants per new home fell from about £120,000 to £30,000. This led to a much greater dependence on housing benefit as households with members in low-income employment, as well as the unemployed and pensioners, needed benefit support to pay the higher rents. This added to the housing benefit bill, which was also climbing dramatically as private rents increased. The government also encouraged through tax incentives both corporate bodies and individuals to participate in the 'buy to let' programme, without considering the impact either on house prices for first-time would-be owner-occupiers or on the quality of the private rented homes to be let. The growth of 'buy to let' contributed to the decline in homeownership and, in fact, jeopardised the government objective of increasing homeownership.

The new government also introduced new powers in the Localism Act 2011 for local councils to introduce their own criteria for applicants to be eligible for council housing, to set council rents to a higher level and to reduce security for new tenants, with a minimum tenancy length of two years. Moreover, housing associations who sought development funding for new rented homes also had to agree to convert a significant proportion of their existing tenants to the higher rents when tenants died or moved on. The government's intention was that these higher rents would fund the new development programme, thus removing the need for any government subsidy. Many of the new measures were justified under the banner of localism, in that they were giving local authorities more freedom to develop appropriate responses to their local housing context, but this freedom effectively removed any notion that there was a minimum standard to which local authorities were required to perform – the safety net of the welfare state became full of holes through which the most vulnerable households could fall. While Malpass (2003) referred to housing as the 'wobbly pillar of the welfare state', by 2015, this pillar had, in fact, been removed altogether.

The Coalition's housing reforms were only one component of its localism agenda. The planning reforms also introduced in the Localism Act 2011 also had significant consequences for the supply of affordable housing. In its 2010 election manifesto, the Conservative Party had made a commitment to abolish the regional planning structure. It was the regional spatial strategies developed by the regional assemblies, though approved by central government, which set local housing supply targets. These had never been popular with county and district councils, the majority of which were Conservative-led, and were viewed as imposing new development on communities that did not want it. The government withdrew support for the growth areas that had been initiated by the previous government's 2003 Communities Plan, taking the view that growth should only take place where it was supported by the local community. Housing targets were seen as a local matter. There was no national perspective on where residential or employment growth should take place. The Localism Act introduced a mechanism for local neighbourhood groups to produce plans for their own communities. This tended to empower groups who oppose new development. In effect, the Coalition government of 2010–15 witnessed the death of strategic planning. While London had a strategic planning authority in the mayor of London, the mayor's powers did not extend to the metropolitan region, and while the mayor supported increased housing development, his focus was on absolute numbers and not on whether new homes were affordable by Londoners. The development programme became dominated by the needs of investors and not by the needs of prospective occupiers. The national housing strategy, *Laying the foundations* (DCLG, 2011), was not a strategy responding to the evidence of housing need, but a list of ad hoc initiatives, many of which had the effect of boosting demand rather than boosting supply. It is also important to consider the change in attitudes to social housing under successive governments.

Scapegoating social housing

In the last three decades, we have seen social housing being blamed for the concentration of disadvantage and the growth of a dependency culture. Social housing tenants have often been scapegoated as the source of the broader ills of current society, from anti-social behaviour and crime to obesity. Politicians have been quick to use the numerous academic studies showing correlations between tenure and data on deprivation, school exam results, crime and obesity to presume causality – that it is social housing that is responsible for the perceived problems. Some reports published by supposedly left-leaning think tanks have fallen into the same trap. This fails to understand that in a numerically declining and increasingly residualised social housing sector, priority is given to households who cannot afford to access market housing and have acute needs in terms of being actually homeless or without stable accommodation or having medical needs.

It is not surprising that many social tenants are poor relative to homeowners (though not necessarily relative to private rented tenants). The lack of access to good schools, health services or leisure facilities is hardly the fault of the social tenants themselves. Moreover, it is not the tenants' fault that there has not been sufficient investment to maintain their homes and the overall environment in which they live. Moreover, in scapegoating estates, we forget that much council housing is in mixed-tenure neighbourhoods, and that within even the poorest-quality estates, after 30 years of council house sales, there is a mixed-tenure community with homeowners and private tenants. Changing tenure does not necessarily change individual behaviour, and while dispersing council tenants may gentrify a neighbourhood, it only further disadvantages the most vulnerable households.

The best way to counter the residualisation of social housing and the spatial concentration of social housing tenants is to radically increase the supply of social housing so that there are homes for more lower- and middle-income working households, as well as households without employment, and to build a significant number of social rented homes in neighbourhoods that are mainly owner-occupied. This is the best way to achieve mixed neighbourhoods and to remove the stigmatisation of social housing tenants through improving their access to the good-quality services and amenities enjoyed by the 'better off'.

The fetishisation of homeownership

We have become obsessed with homeownership. This is largely an English disease, in the sense that other European countries, including Scotland and Wales, do not share this obsession. In England, property ownership has become identified with wealth appreciation, an association not significantly damaged by the house price falls of 2008–10. It is not surprising, therefore, that most households would like to be homeowners. As well as wealth appreciation, homeownership gives households security, so long as you pay your mortgage. The contrast with the rented sectors became more acute as the private rented sector was deregulated, with increasing rents, reduced security and, in some parts of the sector, continuing poor quality. More recently, governments have lessened security and affordability in the social housing sector, increasing the poverty trap for benefit-dependent households trying to get into employment.

We have reached a stage where homeownership is associated with citizenship in a way that recalls the pre-1867 structure of political rights in England, when only property-owners could vote. This argument was endorsed by the Blair and Brown governments, the former introducing a formal government housing policy target to increase the proportion of households who were homeowners, a target not previously pursued by the Thatcher or Major governments. Even Ed Miliband, when he was briefly leader of the Labour Party, stated that selling council homes was a good thing and that Labour should never have opposed it, while the 'left-of-centre' think tank the Institute for Public Policy Research (IPPR) stated in a report that widening homeownership should be a key policy objective for the next Labour government. It is perhaps ironic that this has come at a time, the first time for decades, when homeownership in England is actually in decline. The proportion of households in England who are owner-occupiers is falling.

The failure of the market

The 2008 credit crunch and recession were a clear demonstration that the housing market was not stable and that depending on the market to meet housing demand was not a sustainable option. It was the excess of credit and the wide practice of lending for house purchase without adequate security that was the main reason for the recession in both the US and the UK. Despite the denials of Gordon Brown, the Bank of England and the Financial Services Authority, the British recession was at least partly home-grown rather than being an unpredictable and unstoppable tsunami blown in from the western hemisphere. The practice of Northern Rock, the demutualised building societies and a range of other banking institutions in lending to people who were not able to pay back their loans was irresponsible, just as it was irresponsible for the government to say that the amount of poorly secured credit was not a matter of concern to them. One of the prime functions of a government is to secure a stable economy and control the level of risks for businesses and households. Both Blair and Brown failed in this basic responsibility, even if Brown did help to 'save the world', or at least the Anglo-Saxon economic model, in the aftermath of the collapse.

It is nevertheless curious that most politicians, commentators and academics recognised the extent to which the failure of the market demonstrated that a new approach to housing policy was required. A paper written for COMPASS in August 2008 (Bowie, 2008a), setting out the extent of the paradigm shift and outlining the basis for a new approach, was criticised by a well-respected former housing minister as 'back to the future'. Another exception was the Smith Institute, who published a report in June 2011, *End of the affair: The implications of declining home ownership* (Haywood, 2011), which concluded that:

> the central plank supporting that vision (of a property owning democracy) – rising levels of home ownership – must now come under scrutiny, and with that, the vision itself. In considering a strategic response to what could prove a continuing shift in the balance of tenures. The issue of an alternative vision will therefore inevitably be raised. Such a vision will have to encompass the role of the state, the funding of welfare, and the relationship between housing tenure and the culture of citizenship. It will involve developing new concepts, but it will also involve a clear-sighted application of those new concepts across the full breadth of public policy formation.

The positive functions of social housing

It is necessary to restate the positive purpose of social housing. When the first council homes were developed after the First World War and the programme was expanded under the Attlee government of 1945–51, council homes were to be provided for working households who would otherwise be housed in relatively poor-quality and expensive privately rented homes. It was only with the dramatic reductions in the stock of council housing in the 1980s and 1990s, and with the introduction of a rationing system that gave priority to homeless households and other households with acute housing needs, that the majority of new tenants were households without full-time employment.

For many households, council-owned homes, and, more recently, housing association homes, have been the only basis for a secure and stable life with a reasonable quality of life and decent space standards in a context where many other factors – unemployment or illness – have a negative impact. Social housing is not all concentrated on 1960s' concrete estates, though the overall quality of social housing has declined as better properties, including most family-sized houses, have been sold off under the Right to Buy. Many recently built housing association homes are of a quality equivalent to and sometimes better than some speculative developments. Moreover, social housing is a public asset that can be made available for future generations, and with sufficient investment, can last for 30, 60 or even 90 years. Investing in bricks and mortar for long-term use is a far more effective use of public resources than supporting unregulated private landlordism through ever-increasing amounts of housing benefit. Expanding the programme of social housing, building houses as well as flats, and building in mixed-tenure and mixed-income areas would enable access to social housing to be widened again to include more working households and reduce the stigmatisation of both the tenure and its occupants. We also need to increase the supply of social homes nearer to the main employment centres so that working households can get to work without having to pay high proportions of their income on commuting.

Between the election defeat of 2010 and 2013, the Labour Party kept a relatively low profile on housing policy. The party's focus in government in the two years after the 2008 recession had been on trying to stimulate the housing market though providing financial support for lenders, borrowers and developers, and the Labour Party at the national level provided support for similar initiatives by the Coalition government, for example, the increasing in stamp duty thresholds so that purchasers in lower-value areas were exempt, as well as the Help to Buy initiative, through which the government guaranteed 20% of purchaser deposits, in effect, reducing the normal deposit for a first-time buyer from 25% of cost to 5% of cost – an initiative that did much to stimulate the housing market in some areas of the country but in the context of London, where house prices soon returned to their pre-recession level, did little to make housing more affordable. By May 2013, average house prices in London had reached £500,000, though Help to Buy provided guarantees up to a maximum purchase price of £600,000. Nevertheless, even with the 20% loan guarantee, buying an average-priced property in London would require an income of over £80,000 a year.

Despite the fact that homeownership was falling as incomes did not keep up with house price inflation, the Labour Party, like the Coalition government, focused on incentivising homeownership. Labour-supporting think tanks such as the IPPR also saw homeownership as the key policy objective (Hull, 2012). Meanwhile, the Fabian Society focused on the need for mixed communities (Gregory, 2009). Both think tanks tended to focus on the squeezed middle, the young professionals who were locked out of the housing market and living in the private rented sector or in their parental homes. Little thought was given to the needs of tenants in the local authority or housing association sector whose rents were being increased, and where, in some cases, through estate regeneration schemes, households were actually being displaced. The Resolution Foundation, established by a former policy advisor to Gordon Brown, Gavin Kelly, also published a series of reports focusing on housing options for the 'squeezed middle' (Resolution Foundation/ SHELTER, 2012; Alakeson 2011, Alekason et al, 2013). The solutions focused on institutional investment in the private rented sector.

In 2013, the Labour Party leadership committed itself to a target of 200,000 new homes a year by 2020, that is, the end of the following Parliament. This compared with actual housing completions in England of 108,000 in 2012/13, and an estimated need of between 240,000 and 280,000 a year. The then Labour Leader, Ed Miliband, established a review of housing policy under Sir Michael Lyons, the former chairman of the BBC, to advise on how this commitment could be delivered. A commission of 12 commissioners was established, comprising representatives from various interest groups – the house-building sector, the Town and Country Planning Association (TCPA), the Chartered Institute of Housing and the Planning Officer Society. The group included one Labour councillor and one academic. The group had a series of consultations, though little engagement with the Labour Party's own membership, with organised Labour in local government or with sympathetic practitioners. However, the commission did not commission its own research. Although nominally independent, it worked closely with the Labour Party's political advisors. Its main focus was on how the government could enable the housing market to work more effectively. It worked on the assumption that there would be no increase in the national housing budget under a Labour government and that it could not consider tax reform, including possible changes to property tax. Michael Lyons was especially sensitive on the latter issue, having previously conducted a review of local government functions and finance in 2004 that had proposed a council tax revaluation, only to find that this was regarded as political suicide by the then government (Lyons, 2004).

There were two other assumptions that impacted on the commission's approach: first, that it had to work within the localism agenda that was central to the Coalition government's approach but now endorsed even more enthusiastically by shadow ministers, notably, Hilary Benn, the relatively low-profile shadow communities secretary, and the shadow planning minister Roberta Blackman-Woods; and, second, what could be described as the Barker fallacy – the argument put forward in the 2004 Barker review that an increase in new housing supply would automatically lead to a significant improvement in housing affordability. It is interesting to note that Kate Barker has recently commented that this linkage was not one explicitly contained in the report, but actually an interpretation put forward by then Housing Minister Yvette Cooper as the government's conclusion from the report, and should perhaps be referred to instead as the 'Cooper' fallacy. Whatever the authorship, this fallacy has been the basis of housing supply policy by successive governments since 2004.

When published, the Lyons report (Labour Party, 2014) did include some progressive recommendations. The report recognised the need for a national spatial plan, a recommendation that seems to have been largely unnoticed. The report also included mechanisms to assist economically strong cities and towns in underbounded authorities (authorities with constraining boundaries) to expand to meet growing housing needs, though the suggestion that development should be imposed on neighbouring authorities led to accusations of centralism. The proposal to tax landowners of developable but undeveloped sites led to similar accusations. The report also proposed revolving infrastructure funds. The commissioners also recognised the importance of land assembly, proposing that councils should be able to acquire development sites at existing use value with a generous uplift, though the level of the 'generous uplift' was not specified. The report also recognised that the use of viability appraisals for determining planning applications was problematic and that government guidance on the parameters for assessments was needed.

There were, however, serious deficiencies, which is not surprising given the restricted remit given to Lyons by the Labour Party leadership. There was neither a definition of nor a target for affordable housing. The recommendations still saw increased market housing supply as the key objective. There was recognition that the affordability of new housing should have some relationship with local incomes but there was no recognition that a separate target and separate mechanisms were needed to provide housing that would be affordable by lower-income households without dependence on housing benefit. This was related to the fact that there was no recommendation to the next government as to the level of housing investment. It was noted that this was a decision for a future chancellor, having regard to competing priorities, though Lyons did point out that such investment would be useful. There were no proposals for the reform of the tax system, and an assumption that without new tax revenue, there could be no new investment. Overall, there was a continued over-reliance on the market to deliver. Like Kate Barker 10 years earlier, Lyons thought that the key role for the government was enabling market delivery rather than trying to manage it.

The months before the 2015 general election saw an increasing public debate about the state of housing in England, but much more critically in London, where polling demonstrated that housing had actually become a central political issue (*Evening Standard*, 2015). There was much discussion as to how younger professionals were being excluded from the housing market and considerable focus on the extent to which foreigners were buying up properties in the prime London market for investment as much as for occupation or letting. The Coalition government was forced to change the rules on stamp duty exemption for foreign and corporate purchasers, and to increase stamp duty on higher-value properties. The Labour Party, having previously avoided any discussion of property taxes, then adopted the Liberal Democrats' proposal for a tax on properties with a value of above £2 million, a proposal known as the 'mansion tax'. This proposal proved unpopular with property-owners in London, including those whose properties were worth nowhere near £2 million but who thought that a Labour government would lower the tax threshold, or who actually realised that with property values increasing by 10% a year, their property would cross the threshold in 10–15 years' time and they would be liable. The mayor and many London Labour MPs opposed the proposed tax, with stories of the elderly lady who just happened to live in a £2 million property. When it was pointed out that a person in such a position who had insignificant income could defer the tax so that it became a charge on the sale of the property, the 'mansion tax' was then attacked as a 'death tax'. Understandably, the Liberal Democrats soon dropped their proposal and switched to supporting higher council tax bands for higher-value properties.

When it came to writing the election manifesto, the Labour Party was very non-committal on housing. Having previously announced that Labour would double the number of first-time buyers, without setting out the mechanism for achieving this, Labour made a rather unspecific commitment to more homes for first-time buyers. They also proposed fairer rents for private tenants, having promoted the idea of a three-year standard tenancy (though not necessarily a mandatory one) and some control over rent increases (though no control on initial rent levels or on increases once the three-year tenancy came to an end). Housing was left off the initial Labour Party election pledge card, though by the time the five pledges became chiselled in a stone tablet, a sixth pledge had appeared: 'Homes to Buy and Action on Rents'. When challenged for details, Labour spokespersons would wave a copy of the Lyons report and say 'We have a plan'.

It was the Conservatives who pushed housing to the forefront of the election campaign. They had initially focused on the starter homes initiative, which had been announced in the Budget, but now moved beyond the Help to Buy loan guarantee to a grant to savers of £50 for every £200 saved through a tax-free Housing Individual Savings Account (ISA). Developers could bring forward housing schemes at prices 20% below market value on brownfield sites not previously allocated for housing, and with these homes being treated in planning policy as affordable, they would be exempt from contributing through planning obligations to affordable housing elsewhere and would also be exempt from paying the Community Infrastructure Levy development tax. Labour's response, not wishing to be seen as opposing the aspirations of would-be homeowners or as obstructing additional homes, supported the initiative, with the caveat that the funding invested in Housing ISAs should be used to finance new development – a suggestion that is not that helpful as in order to protect the investors' savings, such reinvestment could only be at market rates of return.

The Conservatives then made a surprise announcement that the Right to Buy for council tenants should be extended to all housing association tenants. This was a proposition that they had first made 23 years earlier only to lose the legislation in the House of Lords. This time, the Conservatives proposed that the right applied to all housing association tenants, subject to a three-year qualifying period, irrespective of whether the homes had received government grants and irrespective of whether the housing associations had charitable status or not. The maximum discount in London was to be £104,000, and £78,000 in the rest of England. The Tories wrong-footed the Labour leadership as Ed Miliband, the Labour leader, had publicly stated that he supported the Right to Buy. The shadow chancellor, Ed Balls, appeared to support the extension to housing associations. Labour was slow to realise that the new initiative was to be funded by requiring councils to sell off their higher-value properties in order to compensate housing associations for the loss of assets from the enforced disposal.

The third Conservative proposal was to reduce the welfare benefit cap from £26,000 a year to £23,000 a year. The Conservatives were aware that cutting benefits was one of their most popular policies and that Labour would not risk the political consequences of defending benefit recipients. While many benefit recipients were working households in low-paid jobs unable to pay increasing rents, they were nevertheless perceived by most of the electorate as undeserving scroungers. The furthest Labour would go was to say that they would hold the benefit cap at £26,000 a year, a level totally inadequate to reflect London's high housing costs.

When the election campaign started, there was little difference between the Labour and Conservative Party positions. Labour felt obliged to support or at least not oppose the series of Conservative announcements. Labour did not focus on the housing issue in the election campaign, partly because they had no distinctive policies that could be seen as potentially vote-winning. Labour could make no commitments on investing in social housing, whether in existing estates or new homes, because it had committed itself to further reducing public spending through its 'triple lock'.

The groups working within and with the Labour Party had little or no influence on the development of policy positions for the manifesto or on the political debate. The national Labour Housing Group published a statement summarising key policies for a Labour government (Labour Housing Group, 2013), while its London group published a detailed policy statement on key issues for housing in London, both to influence the national debate and to set a base position for prospective Labour candidates in the 2016 mayoral election (London Labour Housing Group, 2015). The Labour Finance and Industry Group, another Labour Party-affiliated society that had regular meetings with shadow ministers and their policy advisors, also argued for the party to make commitments to invest in both new social housing and estate regeneration. The Highbury Group on Housing Delivery, the progressive research and policy network established in 2008, was requested by the shadow environment team to set out mechanisms for implementing some of the recommendations of the Lyons review, though this was for use after Labour was in government rather than for any statements during the campaign (Highbury Group on Housing Delivery, 2015).

A separate but related initiative to argue for new social housing had been established by a group around John Healey, the last housing minister in the pre-2010 Labour government. The group, using the acronym SHOUT (Social Housing Under Threat), made an unsuccessful attempt to seek to persuade the Labour Party that it should not focus solely on homeownership. Just before the election, John Healey published with John Perry a paper for the Fabian Society (which had previously not been very interested in the subject), arguing the case for a new social housing programme (Healey and Perry, 2015). This approach was somewhat at odds with mainstream thinking within the Labour Party.

A parallel initiative was undertaken by the Centre for Labour and Social Studies (CLASS), a think tank set up by the trade union UNITE. In the run-up to the election campaign, CLASS published a series of briefing papers for trade union members, with the housing paper taking up much of the Highbury Group's interventionist agenda (CLASS, 2015). There is no evidence that this had any impact on the Labour Party's manifesto or election campaign.

With the Conservatives winning the May 2015 general election and no longer having to rely on the Liberal Democrats, they were in a position to move quickly to implement their proposals to extend the Right to Buy to housing associations and to force councils to sell off high-value properties. Meanwhile, the Labour Party was caught up in a debate over why the election was lost, with a widely held view that the Labour Party was seen not only as not economically competent, but also as too left-wing and not sufficiently recognising the aspirations of working people, including their aspirations to be homeowners. With the resignation of the party leader, Ed Miliband, four out of the five candidates to succeed him took the 'more aspirational' position and argued for the need for economic competence, that is, recognising the need for cuts in spending and welfare benefits. This included dropping the mansion tax proposal and any suggestions for increased taxes for higher earners. Most of the candidates did not appear to recognise housing as a key issue. However, the exception was Jeremy Corbyn, the MP for Islington North and the most left-wing of the candidates, whose anti-austerity agenda included investment in social housing.

At the same time as the Labour Party was choosing its new leader, the Liberal Democrats shifted to a more radical position by replacing Nick Clegg by Tim Farron, with their commitment to a 300,000 homes a year target. More significant, perhaps, was the fact that the Labour Party was also choosing its candidate for the 2016 mayoral elections. With the crisis of housing affordability being most acute in London, housing became the main issue in the initial debates. There was a recognition both of the severity of the housing crisis and the inadequacy of current responses. Candidates with roles in the Blair and Brown governments, either as ministers or as advisors, were now recognising the need for much greater public sector intervention and control of development. However, there were still some serious misunderstandings, for example, Adonis's view in the *City villages* report published by the IPPR (2015) that redeveloping council estates at higher density for market housing would generate the value uplift needed for regeneration, forgetting two key issues: first, that lower-income households actually lived on these estates and may not be that enthusiastic about being displaced; and, second, that value uplift also means price uplift – and that many Londoners would not be able to afford the new homes (Bowie, 2015).

While many of the Act's provisions have not, as yet, been brought into effect, and secondary legislation still requires parliamentary approval, the only hope for delay arises from the fact that with Brexit, the government's attention is elsewhere. The former Housing and Planning Minister Brandon Lewis, who rushed the Bill through Parliament, and who had resisted reasoned amendments, has now moved into another role. He has been replaced by the Croydon MP Gavin Barwell, who has not previously shown interest in the issue, and with new Prime Minister Theresa May seeking to re-establish a One Nation Toryism, there is perhaps a prospect that some of the harsher measures, such as Pay to Stay or the imposition of shorter tenancies, will be watered down in the regulations. In his initial statements, the new minister has sought to argue that housing policy should focus on other tenures and not solely on homeownership.

In the first months after the change in government, dominated by the Brexit aftermath and the second leadership contest in the Labour Party within a year, and with Parliament in its long summer recess, there was little political opposition to the government's policy. The Labour Party does not have the votes in Parliament to block implementation as, with the application of English votes for English laws procedures applying, the government has an effective majority of 100, and the Labour opposition is in disarray. John Healey resigned as shadow housing and planning minister. Whereas John Healey argued against Labour giving a commitment to repeal the Housing and Planning Act, he took the view that Labour needed to rethink its housing policy. However, some indication of a policy shift was given in a speech by Teresa Pearce, MP for Erith and Thamesmead, who was covering the housing and planning remit, to the Labour Party conference on 25 September 2016, in which she announced that Labour in government would: suspend the Right to Buy; remove borrowing limits on local authorities; set up a National Investment Bank and regional development banks; introduce a three-year private rented tenancy; deliver a million homes over the next Parliament, of which half would be 'social housing'; introduce a national housing standard; and reverse the 'Pay to Stay' provisions of the Housing and Planning Act 2016 – a far-ranging programme (Pearce, 2016). The commitment to a million new homes was repeated by Jeremy Corbyn in his leader's speech two days later. Corbyn also said that Labour would 'control private rents' (Corbyn, 2016). How this will be achieved is less clear. Two weeks after the conference, John Healey returned to his previous shadow cabinet role, supported by Teresa Pearce and Ruth Cadbury, the MP for Brentford and Isleworth, so after the hiatus over the summer and early autumn, there is an opportunity for Labour both to oppose the government in Parliament and to develop a coherent alternative strategy on housing supply. One of the purposes of this short book is to move beyond protest and critique to set out a comprehensible and deliverable set of reform measures to overcome the current crisis in the supply of affordable housing in England.

3

THE FAILURE OF GOVERNMENTS SINCE 1979 AND THE IDEOLOGICAL CONTINUITIES

On becoming UK prime minister in 1997, Tony Blair inherited two fundamental ideological assumptions that had driven government policy on housing from the Thatcher/Major period: that homeownership was the essential basis of citizenship and should be promoted; and that the market could be relied upon not just to deliver market housing, but also to enable the provision of affordable housing. The reason for New Labour adopting such basic Thatcherite neoliberal ideological presumptions still remains difficult to understand, and historians can no doubt ponder the extent to which these established principles, though relatively newly established, were adopted by default or by intention. New Labour recognised that Thatcher's introduction of council house sales was a popular policy in winning over the votes of middle-income and 'aspirational' working-class voters and that any proposal to repeal would be an electoral mistake. They accepted the simplistic view that as most poorer households lived in council housing, it was their housing status that conditioned them to dependency and that homeownership would somehow liberate them from this constraint. The government argued that they were responding to consumer choice; if surveys showed that 90% of households wanted to be homeowners, then that proved that homeownership was a good thing, and that in promoting it, the government was doing what the people wanted. Few of the surveys actually asked households whether they could afford to buy a home and whether they thought that they might be able to do so in the foreseeable future.

The Blair, Brown and successive governments have all focused their policies on encouraging more households to become homeowners, creating a range of routes to homeownership, including a succession of schemes targeted at professional middle-income households providing public services, who were defined as 'key workers'. This used up increasing amounts of government investment resources to the extent that by 2006/07, the government, through the Housing Corporation, was funding nearly as many households to buy homes as new rented homes to be available in perpetuity for lower-income households.

The Brown government also encouraged – or at least did not use the Bank of England or the Financial Services Authority to in any way discourage – the availability of mortgages to prospective purchasers on terms that were not sustainable for the borrower or for the lender. Compared with more traditional arrangements requiring a 5% deposit and lending on 95% of property value and assuming a loan of 3.5 times household income, with the credit boom and the widening of mortgage lending beyond the pre-existing building societies, loans of 110% of value on income multipliers of 4.5:1 to 5:1 became commonplace. Moreover, with the government encouraging shared-ownership schemes, initial equities fell from the norm of 50% of initial purchase share to 25% or even as low as 15%, Therefore, marginal homeowners could end up paying up to 50% of their net income for a relatively small share of a small flat, with little hope of staircasing to a greater share, and still paying the rent on the unpurchased equity and the repairs costs – not a very good deal. Yet, the government persuaded both itself and these new 'homeowners' themselves that these households were on the homeownership ladder and were therefore good citizens with a 'stake in the country', even if all they actually owned was a debt to a lender in relation to the toilet and possibly kitchenette in a studio flat. Not content with the fact that the proportion of households who were homeowners had increased from 27% in 1918 to 71% in 2003, the government sought to increase this further to 75% by 2015, a target that does not seem to have been based on any assessment of affordability.

Just as successive Labour ministers, including Ruth Kelly, Yvette Cooper, Hazel Blears and Caroline Flint, saw promoting homeownership as the first priority of government housing policy, they have made the achievement of the second and third priorities – the decent homes target and the provision of new social rented housing – more and more dependent on private sector finance, that is, on market profit. The public sector stock renewal programmes have increasingly depended on the transfer of stock to housing associations or developers, the private finance initiative, and cross-subsidies from profitable private development, sometimes enabled by the demolition without replacement of existing social rented housing. We tend to forget that until the late 2000s, there were direct public sector grants for estate renewal – for example, the Estates Renewal Challenge Fund, the Single Regeneration Budget and the Capital Challenge programmes. With the end of such programmes, and the government's continuing rejection of the 'fourth option' of estate-based reinvestment for improvement or replacement by the local authority, tenants now have no alternative to being pushed down a market-led route, generally involving the transfer of the ownership of their homes with reduced security. The principle of collectively owned and publicly accountable management died a long time ago.

Turning to the third priority, governments have increasingly relied on the market to provide affordable housing. Twenty years ago, the full capital cost of new council housing and housing association housing was funded by government; the public funding – 100% grant –route survived for supported housing into the mid-1990s. As late as 2000, under the mixed finance arrangements introduced under the Housing Act 1984, family-sized social rented schemes in high-cost areas could get 75% of capital costs funded, with rent income, under a regulated rent system, being capitalised to cover the remaining 25% of capital cost. The total cost indicator actually calibrated the grant necessary to meet costs not covered by rent income – with the cost limit driven be real costs in specific areas and increased if costs went up.

For the decade after 2002, we have had: a rent target system that has allowed council and housing association rents to reflect value as well as tenant affordability; an average grant at between 30% and 50% of capital cost (with many new housing association schemes and, in fact, whole areas of the country not getting any grant at all); and a Treasury assumption that even if build costs go up by 5–10% a year, and land costs climb at a much higher rate, housing associations, through 'efficiency savings', can somehow increase output by 7% a year in quantity terms for the same amount of cash, that is, without any inflation allowance. Housing associations are assumed to be 'sweating their assets', which, in practice, means not just using up their reserves, but using receipts from initial equity sales and the staircasing of shared-ownership homes, receipts from development for outright sale, and, in some cases, receipts from the disposal of existing social rented homes – generally those in the highest-value areas – or from cutting management and maintenance costs. The New Labour government and the Housing Corporation also believed that affordable housing can be piggybacked on private housing and that if only local planning authorities were better negotiators, less public subsidy would be needed as developers would provide much, if not all, of the affordable housing required from their profits – they would also help fund the roads, train networks, buses, schools, health centres, parks and the public realm as a whole, so the new sustainable communities would be virtually self-financing.

The Blair and Brown governments believed that all they needed to do was set higher housing targets, make councils grant more planning permissions and the new homes would be built – the more homes were built, the more affordable they would be, and the more social rented and shared-ownership homes would be built. When the housing figures did not go up and prices come down as the government's macroeconomic model said that they should, the government blamed councils for not allocating enough land for housing and not granting enough planning permissions, rather overlooking the fact that consents had increased and that, for example, in London, there were nearly four years' worth of planning consents in the development pipeline. This was when the market was positive and demand, at least for market homes, was strong, even in the northern cities where the government's pathfinders programme was planning to demolish homes to reduce supply in order to increase house prices – always a rather bizarre strategy as prices were going up anyway. It should be noted that the approach of the Cameron government was somewhat different – targets were seen as an obstacle to delivery, though interestingly, in the run-up to the 2015 general election, a national housing output target suddenly reappeared.

The idea of a crude direct relationship between new building completions and house price inflation rather ignored more external economic factors. The Brown government was caught in the contradiction of its own policies. When house prices fall, existing homeowners are unhappy, terrified of negative equity and potential default; if house prices go up faster than the rate of income, fewer prospective purchasing households can afford to buy. Treasury policy focused on trying to defend the status quo – to try to link the rate of house price inflation to the rate of wage inflation – unfortunately, the market did not work quite like that. With the credit crunch of summer/autumn 2008, the government got the worst of both worlds – house price falls and negative equity, but with the credit crunch and the restrictions on lending, homes only became more affordable in theory as less households could afford to buy. A 15–20% fall in prices was of limited benefit to marginal homeowners when their purchasing power had fallen by over 40%.

The consequences of this neoliberal approach to housing have been:

- A sub-market rented programme that depended on both private developers wanting to build and housing associations being able to borrow – two conditions that have become problematic.
- New developments with no funding for social infrastructure, which has further increased the risk of developers being unable to market completed units, and therefore generated a further disincentive to further private investment. The growth areas programme has come

to a standstill, and the government target of 240,000 homes has not been deliverable. England housing starts fell from a peak of 184,910 in 2005/06 to 90,430 in 2008/09 – a fall of 51%. The fall in market sector starts was even greater, from 167,430 to 71,480 – a fall of 57%.

- Estate regeneration schemes are no longer viable as the cross-subsidy from market-led development no longer exists.

- Short-term market demand has generally produced housing that is not appropriate to meeting long-term housing needs. There is an overhang of completed market units, often small units in higher-rise developments, which cannot be sold but are too small or otherwise inappropriate, in terms of location and/or build form, for use as social housing. Developers have often been building for a market that no longer exists, especially with the fall of investors in 'buy to let', so some developers have been in financial difficulty and some new homes have been be left empty. With further difficulties in the property market post-Brexit, there is a risk that some half-built developments, especially those dependent on international investment, will be mothballed.

- Households who had bought homes (or parts of homes) who could not really afford to, and who now have difficulty selling and paying back the mortgage if they want to move. This is not very good for labour mobility. Such households will be at risk of mortgage default if their income falls, and if there is a new recession, mortgage famine or house price fall, this will have a wider negative impact on the economy. The housing market remains volatile, with significant regional variations.

- Increasing affordability issues with social rented homes (or former social rented homes now let at higher rents and the new so-called affordable rented homes at up to 80% of market rents) as the combination of higher rents and service charges means that those households not on benefit are paying higher proportions of their income on housing costs, which acts as a disincentive to seek employment – a point rather misunderstood by Labour Housing Minister Caroline Flint in her 'get a job or lose your "subsidised" home', which is the basis of the new government's 'Pay to Stay' policy. This premise also ignores the point that for many councils, rent income covers costs and therefore generates a surplus that either keeps council tax down or is clawed back by the Treasury.

• Government revenue, widely referred to by ministers as 'taxpayers' money', was used in the context of the Northern Rock and the Royal Bank of Scotland bailouts not to help those in housing need, to stimulate house-building or even to stimulate the housing market, but to take over the risk from mismanaged banks and building societies.

The basic conclusion in relation to the government's response to the recession of 2008 is that the government could not really have got it much more wrong. The belief that house prices would go on rising, that somehow this was good for everybody and that it would somehow provide more affordable housing was not just based on the wrong ideology, but based on a complete lack of logic or analysis. The Treasury's belief, encouraged by the Bank of England Monetary Policy Committee member Kate Barker, that deregulation and the abolition of planning and public sector-led frameworks for development was the solution was always questionable as it was not based on any evidence. Just as was the belief that a new tax, the Community Infrastructure Levy, would fund sustainable communities, or the belief that local authorities, other public bodies or private developers would come to the rescue of affordable housing by providing free land to housing associations. All these initiatives were always just a diversion from, or an excuse for not facing up to, the fundamental deficiencies of market dependence.

The basic Keynesian analysis is that when the market slows down, the state needs to intervene. However, interventions to support specific financial institutions needed to be related to long-term policy objectives. It could be argued that any public sector resources should have been focused on output rather than protecting individual companies and their shareholders from the consequences of their own actions. It is necessary to distinguish between short-term actions and longer-term options.

The Brown government's initial response to the credit crunch in the summer/autumn of 2008 was to try to restore confidence in the banking system. The initial action was to save building societies and banks from collapse by recapitalising – that is, by providing them with significant equity, funded by taxpayers. The government thought that by recapitalising the banks and building societies, they would again provide mortgages to prospective house purchasers. In an attempt to re-stimulate both the housing market and the wider economy, the government reduced the base bank rate in a series of reductions from 5% in October 2008 down to 0.5% in March 2009. However, while encouraging banks and building societies to restart mortgage lending, the government did not make this a condition of its equity investment. The government also extended the exemption from stamp duty for homes below a value threshold of £175,000 to 31 December 2009.

The Homes and Communities Agency (HCA) established in December 2008 to take over the roles of both the Housing Corporation and English Partnerships recognised that if it was to spend its inherited budget, it would need to switch resources from the shared-ownership programme to different forms of rented provision. Some unsold homes were converted to social rent while others were converted to sub-market rent. Some market homes that were completed but unsold were also acquired by housing associations for rented housing. The HCA also made significant pump-priming investment in three stalled estate regeneration schemes in London – the Aylesbury estate in Southwark, Woodberry Down in Hackney and Ferrier in Greenwich. In some cases, grant per new home was paid at a significantly higher level than in the 2007/08 investment programme.

In the April 2009 Budget, the government announced that it was bringing forward future resources to 'kickstart' the development programme. This provided an additional £400 million investment. A further change of tack by the UK government occurred on 29 June 2009. In the announcement 'Building Britain's future' (DCLG, 2009), a further £1.5 billion was made available for new housing investment. However, it should be noted that this was not new money, but resources taken from the government's budget for improving council housing up to the 'decent homes' standard and from the programme for transport and social infrastructure in the growth areas such as Thames Gateway. In some cases, grant per unit was raised to levels of about £200,000 in order to reactivate deferred housing projects, but the total volume of investment was not sufficient to take housing starts back to the pre-recession level.

On 30 June 2009, the government announced the initial findings of its long outstanding review of council housing finance. This included a proposal that councils could keep all the receipts from selling council homes and a proposal that councils could keep surpluses on their housing revenue accounts. In the April Budget, the government announced a new fund of £100 million for councils to undertake direct development; in June, this figure was increased to £400 million. The review of the Housing Revenue Account (HRA) was intended to assist councils who wanted to invest directly in new housing. This represented a significant policy shift from the previous position that all new social housing should be developed by housing associations and that estate regeneration should be undertaken in partnership with private developers or housing associations.

The experience of the first year after the global financial crisis demonstrated that a much more fundamental shift in government policy and a new model for funding affordable housing were required. However, this lesson has not yet been learned. The components of such an alternative approach will be considered in Section Two.

SECTION TWO
THE CRISIS OF HOUSING SUPPLY

4
THE HOUSING DEFICIT

There is now a severe crisis of housing supply in many parts of England, most significantly in London and the South East. The crisis is not just one of a shortage of numerical supply, but one of a shortage of affordable homes. Overall output of new homes has continued to be well below estimates of annual housing requirements. It is generally acknowledged that the annual requirement for new homes is between 240,000 and 280,000 a year, while in the last five years, housing output has ranged between 100,000 and 125,000 a year. The housing requirement in London is assessed at 62,000 homes a year, while output in recent years has ranged between 15,000 and 18,000. For households unable to access market homes, the position is even more acute. Taking London, the area of most acute housing need, where an average market home costs £500,000, more than 18 times average individual incomes of £28,000, more than 50% of households in housing need require some form of sub-market housing – over 30,000 a year – while only 2,000–3,000 housing association and council rented homes a year are built. However, it should be recognised that the housing deficit is no longer limited to London and the South East. Under-occupation and overcrowding have grown in parallel. We are facing a crisis of undersupply, inappropriate supply, unaffordability and ineffective use of the existing housing stock – problems of quantity, quality, access and distribution. The issue of housing affordability will be discussed more fully in Chapter Five. The issue of housing type and quality will be considered in Chapter Six, while the issue of the effective use of both the existing and new housing stock will be considered in Chapter Seven. In this chapter, I will first discuss some of the factors impacting on undersupply before focusing on the issue of where new homes should be built, considering first the challenges of responding to the acute housing shortage in the South East of England, centred on London.

Successive governments have tended to focus on planning policy and practice as the main constraint on housing supply, both in terms of the overall number of new homes built and in terms of the market price. This was the key conclusion of Kate Barker's review of housing supply in 2004. It was not until the recession of 2008 that it was acknowledged that the lack of effective demand in terms of the ability of households to afford to buy and rent properties was also a factor, the recession in 2008 actually being primarily a 'credit crunch' as finance for household purchase was curtailed.

As discussed earlier, the Blair, Brown and Cameron governments also perceived planning as a constraint on housing supply and saw planning as a bureaucratic process that got in the way of developers. Following the 2004 Barker report on housing supply (Barker 2004), there has been a plethora of reports examining perceived obstacles to housing delivery, some of which, such as those from think tanks such as the Policy Exchange, have been based on ideological preconceptions and sometimes fairly crude macroeconomic or process analysis (eg Ball, 2012).

Economic and political factors

The housing market reflects the position in the wider UK economy and is also affected by international economic developments, as was demonstrated with the 2008 recession. However, as the recession also demonstrates, the housing market is itself a key component of the economy. Growth in house prices in both the second-hand market and the market for new homes is driven primarily by consumer demand. However, in this context, especially in relation to the market for new homes, consumers include investors as well as potential occupiers.

Whereas demand for owner-occupation is driven by household incomes, the availability of loan finance and the access of prospective purchasers to savings (whether their own or through inheritance), for investors, different factors apply. Investors may be less interested in income from the rental value of property than in the potential for appreciation in the value of the asset, and the potential of the asset to serve as security for borrowing to support other expenditure. Investment therefore relies on security that a minimum rate of return, either as revenue income or in terms of asset value appreciation, is certain. Investors will therefore compare their potential return with potential returns from other investments (eg in the productive economy or in other services), which may be investments in the UK or investments in other countries, including residential investment elsewhere. In recent years, the UK property market, especially the prime London property market, has become an attractive investment not just for domestic investors, but for international investors. This is because of the relatively high level of asset appreciation, as well as the relatively generous tax treatment of such gains.

The level of investment is therefore affected by UK tax policy. The government can and has used changes in policy on property-related taxes such as stamp duty to either stimulate or restrain the housing market or to stimulate or restrain different components of the market. Policies on capital gains tax or inheritance tax or in relation to the tax treatment of corporate investments also have a significant impact (Edwards, 2015, 2016).

Financing the development sector, land-banking and housing output

Analysis of fluctuations in the output of new housing has generally paid insufficient attention to the operations of house-builders, who have been the main providers of new homes since council house-building effectively stopped in the early 1980s. We are in a situation where 50% of new house-building activity in England is undertaken by 15 house-builders (Payne, 2016). As has been pointed out by Payne, Edwards and others, developers will focus on maximising value rather than on the volume of output and will, in practice, not wish to put more than 50 homes on a single site on the market at the same time as flooding the market depresses sales prices. The issue of whether or not house-builders are land-banking to limit output and maximise price has been a very contentious one. There is good evidence that house-builders do have significant land in the pipeline, albeit that the pipeline is falling relative to build rates. A Savills report in August 2013 on 'UK residential development land' found that while in 2009, a year into the recession, house-builders had consented land for 7.5 years of output, by 2012, the future had fallen to 5.3 years (Savills, 2013; see also Figure 4.1).

Figure 4.1: Developers' landbanks

Permissioned landbanks Top eight housebuilders

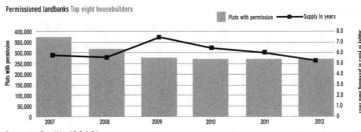

Source: Savills (2013).

Planning approvals for residential development can run at twice annual completions. This has been the case in London for most of the last decade. As at 31 March 2015, it was estimated that there were 139,800 residential units with planning consent that had not started on site. This compared with 156,272 units under construction, and the completions in the previous financial year of 31,818 units (or 27,916 net of demolitions), so the consented pipeline not started on site was equivalent to 4.4 years of output. However, it should be acknowledged that there are factors other than house-builder rationing that slow down output. While there is often a focus on the delays in signing up to planning obligation agreements with the local planning authority, there is often an issue, certainly for major new developments, of phases of development being dependent on transport and social infrastructure being provided, which may be dependent on government funding not yet secured. Developers are not going to commit funds to building unless they know that their homes are marketable, and purchasers may not be enthusiastic about homes in a middle of a building site with no public transport access, no school, no health facilities and no shops. Building housing does not necessarily create a marketable new settlement. There may be good plans for a 'sustainable' community but the implementation of plans needs to be paid for.

However, it does need to be recognised that residential planning consents are often obtained by investors who have no intention of developing themselves, but are interested in increasing the value of their land to sell on at an appropriate time to developers – and the appropriate time is not at the bottom of the market, but when they think value can be maximised. Research for the mayor of London by Molior found that about half of consents were actually on land owned by investors, though further research in July 2014 concluded that the proportion of consented sites owned by house-builders as opposed to investors was increasing (Mayor of London, 2012, 2014).

This, then, brings us to the issue of who finances development. Developers build when they know that they can sell and cover their financing costs. Developers need finance to by land and to prepare the development proposal, as well as to build. Some lessons were learnt from the 2008 recession, where overcommitted developers went bankrupt and were taken over by other house-builders or, in some cases, by the banks from whom they had borrowed (some of whom found themselves owned or partly owned by the British government). The bigger the scheme, the more indebted the developer and the greater the security sought by the lenders, whereas a 15% return was often acceptable pre-recession, developers and their lenders were generally seeking a return of 20% or more post-recession. For high-density and especially high-rise schemes, upfront costs escalated. Not only did land costs and development density rise, but once you start building a high-rise development, you do not really want to stop halfway up waiting for more purchasers.

This explains why developers seek to maximise off-plan sales – off-plan means selling before you start building. For the most costly schemes, developers would seek 40–50% off-plan sales before ordering the pile drivers, never mind the tower cranes. Given that off-plan purchase to completion can take three years or more, these homes are generally not marketed to prospective owner-occupiers (Who wants to wait three to four years to live in the home that they have bought?), but to investors, and in the UK context, especially the London context, where the property market is booming (or at least was until the Brexit vote), this tends to mean international investors. The consequence is that much of the new development market, especially in the case of the prime London market, is targeted not at potential occupiers, but actually at investors. This is a serious problem that has to be deal with. This is perhaps the most extreme example of the commodification of housing – housing as investment rather than for consumption (or, to use more popular terminology, for residence). The prime London market is now a bank for surplus international wealth, and, as Transparency International have demonstrated in their 2015 report *Corruption on your doorstep* (Transparency International, 2015), wealth that often comes from suspect sources.

The cost of land

Land costs are a critical contributor to housing costs and to the unaffordability of the housing market. The land component has been largely ignored in much recent debate on housing policy, although it has long been central to academic discourse (for debates pre-1914, see Bowie, 2016a); for a classic theoretical analysis, see Massey and Catalano, 1978). However, there has been little work on the role of land in planning policy since the work of John Ratcliffe, Nat Litchfield and Yvonne Rydin in the 1970s and 1980s (Ratcliffe, 1976; Litchfield and Darim-Drabkin 1980; Rydin, 1986). This is now changing however. Michael Edwards's (2015) Foresight report on housing pays appropriate attention to the role of land. Peter Hetherington (2015) also recently published *Whose land is our land?*, though the focus is mainly on rural land. Andro Linklater (2015) has also recently published a fascinating book on the history of land ownership in the UK. Furthermore, an analysis of the role of land in housing and economic policy is due to be published by the New Economics Foundation (Ryan-Collins et al, forthcoming).

However, the issue of the impact of land costs and housing affordability remains under-researched, and the lack of a national register of land and the restriction on free public access to land transaction data since the Land Registry was put on a commercial basis (no doubt further restrictions will follow from the proposed privatisation of the Land Registry) has made research on this issue difficult. The contribution of land costs to housing costs is most acute in central London. Analysis undertaken before the 2008 recession demonstrated the costs of housing land in London ranging from £3 million per hectare to over £300 million per hectare. With agricultural land values at £26,560 per hectare (£10,750 per acre) (RICS, 2016), a farmer whose site is zoned for housing by the local planning authority realises a massive uplift in value. For the owner of an urban warehouse or factory site, the value uplift from housing zoning will be less but still significant. A key challenge is therefore how to ensure that development land suitable for housing is brought forward for development at the lowest possible cost. Suggestions made by some, for example, the House of Lords Economic Affairs Committee (House of Lords, 2016), that taxing land suitable for development will encourage landowners to bring land forward to the development market, will just add to the cost of housing land.

Government subsidy

Historically, social housing has been funded primarily through government grant, rather than relying on cross-subsidy from private developers, either directly or through planning obligations. From the mid-1980s, funding operated on the basis of what was known as the mixed funding regime, by which housing associations received grants to fund that proportion of capital costs of new homes that could not be met from rent income, which was, in effect, capitalised over a 60-year period. Housing associations only needed borrow finance against this rent income and so did not depend on cross-subsidy from developers or planning obligation contributions, or from receipts from shared ownership or open market sales. This proved to be a very effective mechanism for combining public and private sector finance, with minimum risk to the associations and their tenants' security (Whitehead and Williams, 2015).

In the 1990s and early 2000s, successive governments increased the proportion of the national housing investment budget channelled through the then Housing Corporation, which was to support homeownership initiatives, primarily, shared-ownership housing, as opposed to social rented homes. These arrangements continued when the Housing Corporation was incorporated into the new Homes and Communities Agency (HCA) in 2008. On coming to power in 2010, the Coalition government decided to stop funding social rented homes and instead switch the funding to the misnamed 'affordable rented' programme, with rents up to 80% of market rent. These rules also applied to London when the London proportion of the HCA budget was transferred to the mayor of London in April 2012, though Mayor Boris Johnson decided to aim for average rents at 65% of market rent rather than 80%.

Before the change in policy, investment grant could fund 60–70% of the cost of a new dwelling – in a high-cost area such as Inner London, this could be between £150,000 and £200,000 a dwelling. Under the new regime, this fell to an average of £30,000. In many parts of the country, no grant was available at all. The government's approach was to maximise the unit output for the budget available, and the budget was cut in successive years by both Labour and Coalition governments. Housing associations increasingly focused on schemes not dependent on grants – schemes with higher rents or schemes for market sale. Some entered into partnerships with developers in an attempt to benefit from planning policy requirements and planning obligations imposed by councils on private developments. Many of the larger associations assumed that the future would be without grants. Many middle-sized associations merged or were subsumed into larger associations. Most of the smaller associations had stopped developing in the mid-1990s when the Housing Corporation introduced minimum volume output criteria for organisations seeking funding.

The approach of minimising grants and requiring housing associations to increase rents for new schemes to close to market levels had been predicated on the assumption that housing benefit 'would take the strain' – a policy of revenue grants to households to pay for higher rents on properties that they could not otherwise afford, in contrast with the previous regime that kept rents down and reduced dependency on housing benefit through higher levels of capital subsidy. The recent increases in benefit costs have not been because there are more new lettings or because more tenants are unemployed, but because rents have increased faster than incomes and because more households in lower-paid employment now need housing benefit. The Conservative government has now decided that it will not fund a rented programme even at higher rents, so except for a residual programme for supported housing for people with special needs, all the budget for the next three years will be used to support homeownership, primarily through the new starter homes initiative, with homes for sale at up to 80% of market value. In effect, the grant-free world anticipated by the housing association movement is now with us.

Planning obligations and the Community Infrastructure Levy

As government investment in housing has reduced, so has the reliance on developer contributions to fund both sub-market housing and the transport and social infrastructure to support major new settlements. While the use of planning obligations (often known in England as section 106 agreements in relation to section 106 of the Town and Country Planning Act 1990) is sometimes seen as a mechanism used by central government and local authorities to promote mixed-tenure neighbourhoods and 'balanced communities' the system has been increasingly used primarily to replace public funding. With the reduction and then withdrawal of government grants, as discussed in the previous section, both local authorities (who retained statutory housing responsibilities) and housing associations as providers increasingly relied on planning contributions extracted from private developers through councils using their planning powers. Where a local authority has a target that a proportion of new homes should be some form of sub-market housing (social rent, sub-market rent, shared ownership or some form of discounted market housing), which is based on its strategic housing market assessment, it can require a developer to provide a mix of homes that accords with its policy.

Section 106 agreements are a means of ensuring that a scheme is policy-compliant. Where it may be inappropriate or less cost-effective to provide the affordable housing within a proposed development, the council can take a contribution 'in lieu' of on-site provision to fund affordable housing on another site. This may be appropriate where the proposed development is high-density and includes few family-sized units or involves high service charges that would, in practice, exclude lower-income tenants even if rents were kept relatively low. In the past, section 106 agreements have been useful in supplementing government grants where costs were higher than normal or where significant social infrastructure was required. However, with the reduction of government housing grants and reductions, under successive governments, of government investment for transport infrastructure, schools and health and leisure facilities, section 106 agreements have become a key source of funding, in some cases, the only source, not just for new sub-market homes, but also for transport and social infrastructure. However, even in areas where the need for affordable housing is acute, planning obligations have been increasingly used to fund transport and social infrastructure and less to support sub-market housing. In the London case, research has demonstrated that on strategic housing schemes, while the original London Plan objective was to split section 106 contributions roughly equally between affordable housing and transport, by 2011, over 80% of contributions were going to transport (London Assembly, 2012). This was primarily because, following the principles of transport-oriented development and the London Plan, policies linked residential density to transport capacity, so improving transport links was a precondition for higher-density residential development.

The introduction of the Community Infrastructure Levy (CIL) by the Coalition government was intended to simplify these arrangements by introducing a fixed levy on individual developments to support local authority-wide infrastructure programmes. The government had an unfounded belief that developers were sitting on a pot of gold that could fund affordable housing and social and transport infrastructure, and that section 106 was not extracting enough of this. The government's view was that if developers could self-fund major new settlements, then the government would not need to. The fact that this assumption coincided with the global financial crisis and the reduction in property values was perhaps a little unfortunate. Moreover, CIL was introduced in addition to section 106, not as a replacement for it as the house-builders had anticipated. Moreover, as a fixed-rate tax, CIL, unlike a section 106 agreement, could not be flexed in relation to the development economics of a specific development proposal, so there was a risk that for some schemes, the additional tax would hit the developer's return. The government responded to this concern by stating that neither a council's policy requirements nor their planning obligations or CIL should reduce either landowners' or developers' returns beyond what was reasonable – reasonable not being defined. In practice, this meant that it became increasingly difficult for councils to use planning obligations to fund affordable housing and especially social rented housing. The government's redefinition of affordable to include any form of sub-market housing and new requirement under the 2016 Act for 20% of new homes to be starter homes at up to 80% of market value have made it even more difficult for councils to use planning obligations effectively. The issue of the increased focus on developers' returns and the role of viability assessments will be discussed further in Chapter Eight.

Location and form of new development

In considering the location and form of new residential development, it is useful to consider the different components and to set out preconditions for new settlements. The perspective of the current government is that new settlements should only be developed where there is support from existing communities. This should not be the determining factor. Many reports, including some recent reports by the Town and Country Planning Association (eg TCPA, 2012) advocating new 'garden cities' or 'garden suburbs', are insufficiently explicit about the preconditions that should be met in terms of development location. Ministers, in issuing statements on 'locally planned large-scale development', have not been specific about preconditions, though there is an implication that part of the reason for the failure or at least limited progress of the eco-towns programme is attributable to the top-down approach adopted for site selection. The garden cities concept is often counterposed to the compact city concept. Both garden cities in the pre-First World War period and new towns in the post-Second World War period were proposed as a way of reducing overcrowding in London and other metropolitan centres. The compact city argument, and the urban concentration and densification envisaged, is often put forward as the best way of avoiding urban sprawl and residential development in the countryside. It is useful, however, to examine the advantages and disadvantages of different forms of settlement.

The best approach to the debate about the appropriate form for new development is therefore to set out what the fundamental preconditions are for the delivery of new settlements:

- Identification of land suitable for development in terms of being in an appropriate location, with mechanisms to ensure that the land is brought forward for development.
- A regulatory regime and code of standards which ensures that the homes built are appropriate to meet the requirements of the intended occupiers.

- New developments should only be built in locations where there is access to employment opportunities, transport and social infrastructure, and open space, as well as where there is a mechanism in place to ensure their delivery.
- A funding regime, either in terms of capital or revenue subsidy, which ensures that homes are affordable by the households for whom they are intended.
- A mechanism for ensuring that resources in terms of land, development capacity and construction materials are used efficiently. This can include density controls, the licensing of development and/ or occupation, and financial controls, including taxation measures that disincentivise the underuse of land and residential property.

In applying these principles to a specific development, it is important to stress the importance of ensuring that the location and form of a development should support a wide range of types of housing provision in terms of household type and household income and should be inclusive not exclusive. It is critical that the form of development should be predicated on meeting a range of housing needs rather than being focused on one sector of the market. These factors therefore have a critical impact on identifying suitable locations for development, as well as the built form of development. While the early garden cities were intended to be substantially self-contained, it is perhaps no longer realistic to assume that a large new development can achieve a substantive degree of self-containment in terms of limiting the relationship to other communities through the on-site provision of all employment opportunities for the resident population, together with all the commercial, retail and social infrastructure required. In including relatively isolated sites for significant residential development (such as disused airfields or surplus army barracks), with no existing employment opportunities or public transport networks, the original eco-towns programme did not necessarily ensure that the developments would be self-sufficient, and, in fact, would have created a dependence on the use of private transport for access not just to employment opportunities, but also to social infrastructure. It is therefore critical that in proposing approaches to new large-scale developments, a certain form of development is not necessarily assumed and that a range of locational options are investigated in terms of assessing potential social, economic and environmental outcomes. In this context, while the criteria originally set in *Planning policy statement 1: Eco town supplement* (ODPM, 2009) that new developments should be a minimum of 5,000 homes, *and* be proximate to a higher-order centre where there is a clear capacity for public transport links, *and* be proximate to existing and planned employment opportunities are important, it should be recognised that these criteria can be met through urban extensions or the development of major urban brownfield sites, as well as through garden city developments.

It should be acknowledged that the concept of a self-contained garden city is of little relevance given the inability of government at any level to guarantee employment provision in a specific location, though it should be recognised that an active policy of directing or subsidising employment provision at specific locations is a policy operated in the past that could be reconsidered. Town extensions are fundamentally more viable than standalone projects because of the shared infrastructure that they can benefit from. There is no justification for having a specific set of standards applicable to 'eco-towns', 'garden cities' or 'garden suburbs' that do not apply to other forms of new residential-led development.

Infrastructure

The planning and implementation of such large-scale development requires time (up to five to 10 years) and significant upfront funding. The then Housing Minister Grant Shapps was confident that the financial incentive of the new homes bonus that he introduced in 2011 would be sufficient to encourage support for new development by local authorities, and that the availability of public land brought into joint venture partnerships would draw in private finance. He was also clear that no additional subsidy would be available for new development.

The Coalition government's view was that creative financial models, for example, borrowing on the future value of land uplift or against the new homes bonus, would leverage development capital. They also talk about 'joined-up thinking' within the ministries or a one-stop shop to better synchronise the long-term planning of central government infrastructure funds and planned new development areas.

It is critical that new residential development, whether in the form of garden cities or garden suburbs, urban extensions, or infill development, provides mixed and balanced communities that are sustainable in social as well as environmental and economic terms. This means that they need to include homes that are affordable by lower- and middle-income households, as well as households able to afford to buy homes on the open market. We have a concern that within some current major developments, the range of homes under construction is focused on homes towards the upper end of the market. It is also important that we use the identified development capacity to meet the needs of a range of household types. One of the objectives of new development should be to seek to reduce un-met housing need, and this relates to the needs of households who are unlikely ever to be able to access market housing, as well as the needs of marginal homeowners.

Any tenure model has to respond to the significant affordability gap that we now have between those who already have equity and those who do not. Those without equity will find it increasingly difficult to purchase a home. There is a widely supported case for re-establishing a strong social and private rental sector. This should include dwellings of all sizes for which there is effective demand, and should include houses as well as flats and maisonettes. There also needs to be flexibility for households and properties to switch between tenures. Any development brief needs to be based on an analysis of both housing need and effective housing demand, but needs to be flexible in terms of allowing responses to changing need and demand. This is especially the case for schemes that will take five or more years to be built.

We suffer from extremely low build-out rates, based around sales rates – the impact of which is twofold: first, it increases the cost of development through prolonged 'prelims' and site financing; and, second, it prevents higher volumes of delivery and restricts choice. In many cases, it will not be possible to finance an appropriate proportion of affordable homes, including social rented homes at target rents, solely from the profits of market-led development. Clearly, the availability of land, either at nil cost or at agricultural land value, will assist the provision of affordable homes. It is important to ensure that appropriate land is brought forward for development at low cost. The availability of land at low cost was one of the fundamental reasons for the early garden city developments being viable. Local authorities need to be able to acquire land at close to agricultural or other existing use value, and compulsory purchase powers need to be amended to facilitate this. Nevertheless, even with subsidised land, in many locations, some form of direct public subsidy to development costs will be required if a full range of housing provision is to be achieved. It is also important to stress that the 'appropriate proportion' and form of affordable housing should be determined primarily by the evidence of need for housing in a specified location, and not solely by the development economics of a scheme at a certain point in time. In this context, the references to 'willing landowner', 'willing developer' and 'competitive returns' in the National Planning Policy Framework (NPPF) are unhelpful. A mechanism for funding the provision of social infrastructure is critical to the success of any new residential community. One of Ebenezer Howard's fundamental principles was the trustification of assets so that the appreciation in value could be recycled to provide social infrastructure and other benefits for the community as a whole. One option is for the local authority or a specially established publicly accountable body to take equity in any new development (irrespective of whether the development was on land originally in public or private ownership). The option of establishing a local infrastructure fund could be considered, which would enable infrastructure to be funded by a combination of public sector, institutional, private and individual investment.

Preconditions for new sustainable communities

Before considering the appropriateness of specific locations for new settlements or individual new developments, it is important to set out some basic preconditions. While there have been numerous reports, both historic and more recent, advocating garden cities and garden suburbs, the following preconditions are perhaps the most critical if our definition of sustainability is to incorporate social and economic sustainability, as well as environmental sustainability. It is also important to reiterate that there is sufficient land to meet England's projected housing requirements without concreting over the countryside as long as we both plan development in appropriate locations and ensure that the completed development is used efficiently and appropriately (GOS, 2010). The preconditions for new sustainable communities are as follows:

- Any new settlement needs to be near to employment opportunities that are accessible by public transport.
- Any new settlement needs to include a range of housing types that are affordable by a range of households, including good-quality housing affordable by lower-income households, in order to achieve a genuine mixed and balanced community.
- Any new settlement needs to be supported by accessible social infrastructure – education, health and leisure facilities, including pubs, cafes, places of worship and a library.
- Any new settlement needs to include, and any new development needs to be within walking distance of, a district centre that includes a range of shops.
- Any new settlement requires a comprehensive utilities infrastructure – power supply, water supply and sewage and waste disposal.
- Any new settlement needs to be a place where people choose to live, rather than being an imposed choice as the only option available as alternative options cannot be accessed.

- Any settlement needs to seek to achieve the most effective use of natural resources, both in terms of development and long-term occupation.

For these preconditions to be achieved, a number of factors need to be in place:

- The land needs to be available for development at a price that does not obstruct the delivery of a mixed and balanced community.
- The development must be comprehensively planned in the wider public interest rather than just in the interest of the landowner, developer or investor.
- A regulatory regime must be in place to ensure that minimum standards of residential and related development are achieved, and, where possible, exceeded, while ensuring that homes are affordable by a range of households.
- Sufficient public and private funding must be in place for these objectives to be delivered and this funding must ensure the adequate management and provision of services in the long term as well as the initial capital investment.
- The governance of a new settlement, both in the development phase and post-completion, should be through a democratically accountable body.
- As the asset value of the settlement increases over time, the value should be reinvested in the maintenance of and, where appropriate, the extension of the settlement, rather than enabling private profit.

In considering the implementation of any development strategy, it is important to recognise two key limitations: first, that planners may plan but do not have the powers or funding to direct implementation and ensure delivery; and, second, that the development market, private finance and asset ownership are largely unregulated. There is a third limitation, one that the government has chosen to establish: that there is no government policy on where residential or employment growth should be focused and, consequently, that growth is primarily a matter for the self-determination of each locality.

It also needs to be recognised that current governance arrangements are inadequate. With no structure of regional planning beyond the Greater London Authority boundary, there is no organisational basis for the review of the growth demands of the greater South East and the capacity to meet them. There is already evidence of Home Counties districts failing to collaborate on the politically sensitive issue of balancing demand and capacity at sub-regional level. Ministers have no will to intervene, and while the last mayor of London initiated a preliminary wider discussion, there is still neither a sense of urgency nor a mechanism for the comprehensive review that is required. The perspective of Mayor Boris Johnson that for the following 10 years at least, London's needs could be met within the London boundary, a perspective that appears to be shared by his successor, Sadiq Khan, does not recognise that we need to start our longer-term planning now.

The green belt remains a contentious issue. It is essential that any consideration of the use of green-belt land for development is the result of a comprehensive review of existing land use and development capacity. An unplanned incremental approach to peripheral development based on responses to specific development pressures could be damaging not just to the environment, but to broader issues of economic and social sustainability.

Any strategic framework also has to take into account the potential growth opportunities generated by new infrastructure, notably High Speed 1, High Speed 2, Crossrail 1 and even the potential Crossrail 2, together with orbital transport improvements and more localised projects. These developments have a major impact on whether or not specific locations are viable as significant new settlements.

Any assessment of a development option should therefore have regard to both sets of criteria, as well as to the constraints on implementation. The factors that need to be in place will vary between different locations. Wholly new settlements in the traditional form of garden cities or standalone new towns will generally have a higher cost in terms of ensuring both transport and social infrastructure. With no government strategic policy for the location of employment capacity, providing access to employment opportunities without dependence on private transport (with its negative environmental consequences) will be challenging.

At a time of a shortage of resources to fund significant new infrastructure, there is a strong argument for focusing on new settlements that are accessible to existing employment opportunities and existing social and utilities infrastructure. Consequently, urban extensions and infill suburban development may have advantages and can be more cost-effective and sustainable than relatively isolated new settlements and will be able to provide a wider range of housing types on a more affordable basis than higher-density or hyper-dense developments in metropolitan central locations (such as central London) or in town centre locations, whether within suburban London or the wider metropolitan region, or within areas on the edge of it (Bowie, 2016b, 2016c).

Medium-density development close to existing infrastructure is a much more sustainable form of development and produces a better quality of life for residents than either hyper-dense development in high-rise flats in central London or 'garden city'-type developments in relatively isolated locations, with expensive homes and access to limited employment opportunities. In terms of meeting social, economic and social sustainability criteria, it is likely that three forms of development could make a significant contribution to meeting London's housing requirements: incremental suburban intensification; urban extensions on the fringe of London; and extensions to existing urban centres in the Greater South East that have good transport access to London and/ or have a local employment growth capacity. In each case, it is critical that developments include a full range of built forms and housing types in terms of size, tenure and affordability if further social polarisation is to be avoided.

It is therefore important that we consider a much wider range of development options and focus on what is actually deliverable and what will be delivered in the current funding and market context, and to identify and assess the capacity of individual locations in terms of the criteria specified earlier. This is an exercise that requires some nationally applicable guidance and national government support. New settlements have to be planned within their locational context.

However, this requires coherent national/inter-regional, regional and sub-regional strategies that incorporate housing, economic, transport and environmental components. For such strategies to be developed and implemented, we need government support and intervention, as well as forms of strategic planning and governance structure that are democratically accountable and more effective than the current structure of local enterprise partnerships and the duty to cooperate provisions of the Localism Act 2011. For London and the Greater South East – the London metropolitan region – we urgently need to consider options for a metropolitan region planning and governance structure.

5
AFFORDABLE BY WHOM?

Chapter Four focused on the overall shortage of homes, discussed some of the factors impacting on the production of new homes and set out criteria for deciding where new homes should be built. However, it has been argued in previous chapters that increasing overall supply through a new-build programme only has a relatively marginal effect on the affordability of the overall housing supply. The key challenge is therefore how to ensure that both new and the existing housing supply is affordable by a much wider range of households. With house prices and rents in most parts of the country increasing much faster than household incomes, it is not surprising that the proportion of household incomes being spent on housing has increased dramatically. Housing costs are now a significant component of inequality both between households and between different parts of the UK. Ownership of housing is a critical component in household wealth, and as property values increase, the differential between homeowners (especially those who have paid off their mortgages) and renters becomes more acute (Atkinson, 2015).

Part of the difficulty in having a sensible debate about affordable housing is the increasing abuse of the term 'affordable'. Governments of recent years have tended to use the term 'affordable' as synonymous with 'sub-market'. There was therefore an assumption that affordable housing needed some form of subsidy to be sub-market. However, as house prices have increased far more rapidly than incomes, access to market housing has become far more restricted, and in many locations, property prices and rents have to be significantly below market levels to be accessible to households on average incomes. There are, of course, significant area variations, with average house price to average income ratios being highest in London, the South East and South West. Governments have increasingly tried to find ways of making unaffordable housing more affordable without any direct form of government subsidy.

In the *National planning policy framework* (DCLG, 2012) published by the government in March 2012, the definition of 'affordable housing' for planning purposes was amended to include the new category of 'affordable rented' homes, now part-funded by the government through the Homes and Communities Agency (and in London, through the mayor of London). These are rented homes with rents up to 80% of market rent, with minimum security of tenure of two years – rents much higher than rents for pre-existing council and housing association social rented homes, in which tenants, in effect, had security of tenure so long as they paid their rent. The government has now stopped funding social rented homes at controlled rents (known as target rents). In London, Mayor Boris Johnson is proposing to remove the separate target in the London Plan for social rented homes, which had been 35% under Livingstone between 2004 and 2008, with an indirect target of 25% introduced by Johnson in 2011. Many local authorities are following the mayor's lead – the argument being that if the government considers 'affordable' rented homes to be affordable and equivalent to social rented housing, and the government is no longer funding social rented homes, then there is no point in having a target for social rented homes even if the need for them is proven. Nine London boroughs, including the Conservative-controlled boroughs of Westminster and Kensington and Chelsea, have rightly objected to the mayor's proposal, and at the recent public examination of the proposal, the objectors put forward a very convincing argument that the new policy should not be introduced as it would force thousands of lower-income households to move out of inner London.

For the last few years, at least in London and the South East, we have had an increasing proportion of so-called affordable homes actually being shared-ownership or sub-market rented homes only affordable by households on incomes over £60,000 a year – nearly twice the average household income. London households moving into new 'affordable rented homes' will pay an average rent including service charge of £9,500 a year (£183 a week), compared with the average market rent for market homes of £14,455 a year (£278 a week) (GLA, 2016). It is therefore important to be clear what we mean by affordable housing. While, as house prices continue to increase, there is clearly a demand from middle-income households for homes at 60–80% of market prices and rents, that does not reduce the need for housing at social rents that take up less than 30% of a low-income household's income, the original affordability definition in the London Plan, rather than 40–60% or more.

The government now measures affordability on the ratio of house prices to income. Historically, the benchmark is that average house prices should be no greater than 3.5 times average household income, on the basis that this ratio is generally regarded as a safe lending ration for mortgages for house purchase. The most recent data published by the government – for 2015 – demonstrates the wide geographical variations in affordability. Comparing lowest-quartile house prices with lowest-quartile incomes, there are very few authorities below the 3.5 threshold, an example being Burnley, at 2.71. In London, only one authority falls below 10.0 – Barking and Dagenham, at 9.02. For central London authorities, the affordability ratios are extreme: 30.65 for Kensington and Chelsea and 27.9 for Westminster. The government also compares median house prices with median incomes. For a higher-price area such as Kensington and Chelsea, this actually increases the ratio, while in lower-price areas, this eases it slightly – for example, to 7.50 in Barking and Dagenham. For the most affordable area on the first measure – Burnley – this measure actually increases the ratio to 3.65. The only area below the 3.5 threshold on the latter measure is, in fact, Copeland in Cumbria, at 2.85 (DCLG, Live Tables: Housebuilding, 2016a).

However, it is also important to examine the dynamic of affordability ratios. For England as a whole, the affordability ratio for median house prices to median incomes rose from 3.54 in 1997 to 7.63 in 2015. The ratio for lowest-quartile house prices to lowest-quartile incomes rose from 3.57 to 7.02 over the same period, in effect, homes were nearly twice as expensive relative to incomes as they were 20 years ago. To take the extreme case of Kensington and Chelsea, the affordability ratio has trebled, not just doubled, over this period. In this context, it is not surprising that the proportion of households who are owner-occupiers has fallen and that the average age of a first-time buyer has increased significantly. The UK owner-occupied housing stock fell from a peak of 18.184 million in 2008 to 17.712 million in 2014 – in proportionate terms, this was a fall from 67.4% of the total stock to 63.2%. Data on households (as opposed to dwellings) show a fall from a peak of 71% of households in 2004 to 64% now. The greatest fall in homeownership was in Outer London, where the proportion fell from the peak of 72% in 2000 to 58% in 2016, and with an increase from 12% to 25% of households privately renting over the same period (Labour Force Survey, quoted in Resolution Foundation, 2016). A recent review by the Halifax building society gave an average age of first-time buyers in the UK as 30, with 32 in London. The average deposit in the UK was £33,960, but the London average was three times higher at £95,693. The most affordable homes were in Northern Ireland and Scotland (Halifax, 2016).

Increases in housing costs have not just been limited to the purchase of homes for owner-occupation. Costs to occupants have also increased in the private rented and social housing sectors. Average council rents went up from £19.01 per week to £82.44 per week between 1988/89 and 2013/14 – an increase of 334%. For London, the figures were £22.06 and £102.48, respectively, representing an increase of 360%.

The majority of new housing association tenants now have rents set as a proportion of market rents. For 2014/15, a tenant on a traditional housing association rent paid an average of £86 per week; however, a tenant on an 'affordable rent' paid an average of £117 per week – or 36% higher – this was 30% below the average market rent. The figures varied significantly between regions: in London, housing association rents were £118, with 'affordable rents' being £163; while in the least expensive region, the North West, the figures were £76 and £95, respectively. Private sector rents now average £170 per week in England, with a figure of £368 per week in London.

An alternative approach to affordability than examining house price to income ratios is to analyse the proportion of income that households spend on housing. This also allows for a consideration of the relative costs for households in different tenures and widens the discussion from the rather narrow perspective of marginal homeownership, which has been the focus of government policy over the last three decades. Recent work by the Resolution Foundation (2016) is very helpful in this respect, with Figure 5.1 showing how affordability has changed over time for each tenure, and that for private renters and social tenants, the proportion of net income spent on housing is now increasing.

Figure 5.1: The dynamic of affordability and tenure

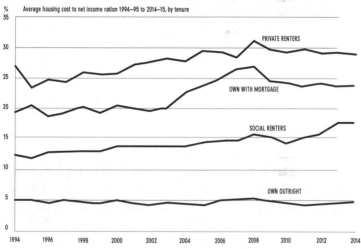

Source: Resolution Foundation (2016).

These national figures hide wide regional variations: in London, the average proportion of net income spent on housing has increased from 21% to 28% since 1994/95; while in the lowest cost region of North East England, the proportion has increased from 14% to 17%. The Resolution Foundation analysis also shows the changes in proportionate housing costs by age group, demonstrating the extent to which younger households have been disadvantaged (see Figure 5.2). It is generally private renters in the lower and middle age groups who are spending the highest proportions of their income on housing.

Figure 5.2: Generational affordability

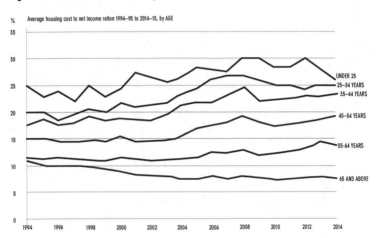

Source: Resolution Foundation (2016).

Recently published analysis from the Office for National Statistics (ONS) shows the extent to which the difficulty that households have in accessing the housing market has led to a significant increase in the number of young adults (15–34) living with their parents (see Figure 5.3). There has also been a significant increase in the number of multi-family households (see Figure 5.4). Additionally, there has also been an increase in overcrowding, with 5.5% of households under 45 being overcrowded, compared with less than 1.5% of households over 55. There is therefore clear evidence that the housing supply deficit is increasing, with an increasingly acute shortage of homes affordable by lower-income households, and that this has severe negative impacts on the quality of life of thousands of households across the country.

Figure 5.3: Young adults living with parents

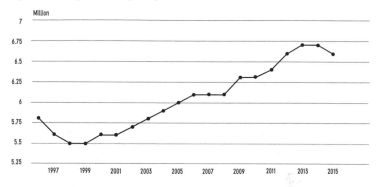

Source: ONS (2015).

Figure 5.4: Multi-family households

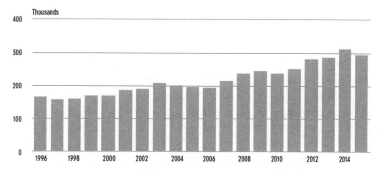

Source: ONS (2015).

6
THE WRONG KIND OF HOMES

Built form and density

In the last two decades, we have witnessed a significant change in the nature of new development, as well as a dramatic increase in the density of new developments. This follows from a range of factors: the wish to protect the countryside and open space in urban areas and, critically in the case of the London metropolitan region, the priority given to the protection of the green belt. Government data show an increase in average development density from 25 dwellings per hectare (dph) in 1996–99 to 42 dph in 2008–11. However, it is also driven by house-builders seeking to maximise profit by getting as many new homes onto a plot of land as they are allowed (see DCLG 2016a, Live tables land use change statistics [unfortunately, this data set is no longer maintained]). Some of the most significant increases are shown in Table 6.1.

In London, densification has proceeded at a much more rapid rate. For 2014/15, average density for completed schemes was 123 dph, but the schemes given planning approval that year increased to 159 dph. In a number of boroughs, average development density was substantially higher than that, for example, Tower Hamlets at 461 dph, Islington at 405 dph, Hackney at 389 dph and Lambeth at 355 dph. These borough averages can include individual developments at densities of over 2,000 dph, equivalent to densities in central Hong Kong. London does have

Table 6.1: Density of new development in dwellings per hectare

	1996–99	2008–11
Liverpool	37	79
Manchester	40	88
Salford	31	118
Leeds	25	61
Sheffield	25	80
Birmingham	37	67
Nottingham	47	84
Leicester	32	61
Plymouth	32	63
Bristol	48	97
Southampton	41	95
Brighton	50	111

explicit guidance on density policy within the London Plan, based on the principles of sustainable residential quality (SRQ), but in nearly every year since the London Plan was adopted in 2004, more than 50% of developments granted planning consent have been above the recommended density (see London Plan Annual Monitoring Report 12, 2014/15; Mayor of London 2016, p 21).

Given concerns as to the erosion of the green belt, it is perhaps significant to note that in the period 2013–16, only 3% of new residential development was within the green belt (DCLG live table 311 DCLG, 2016a). Between 2013 and 2015, 42% of residential development was on land that was not previously developed (often misleadingly referred to as 'greenfield land', while 58% was on previously developed land. The policy of protecting the green belt and seeking to make use of previously developed land before using 'greenfield' land has been a contributing factor to the increase in development densities – 97% of development in London is on previously developed land (London Plan Annual Monitoring Report 12, 2014/15; Mayor of London 2016, p 18).

These increases in density reflect a change in the built form of homes. Data are no longer available at a national level as to the proportion of new development that is flats rather than houses, but with the concentration of development in urban areas, the proportion of development that is flatted has clearly increased. Data for London show that whereas 50% of new homes had been houses a decade ago, that figure has fallen to below 10%. However, what is perhaps most significant, and certainly visible, especially in the London context, is the number of new developments that are primarily high-rise. In the mid-2000s, only a few new residential developments were of 10 stories or more. Recent research estimates that there are more than 400 developments with residential buildings of 20 stories or more in the development pipeline in London (Bowie, 2010a; New London Architecture and GL Hearn, 2016).

The size of new homes

The recent development programme has not been providing the type of homes needed in terms of size. We have not been building enough family-sized homes, and many of the homes that we have been building are very small. There is now no assessment of the nation's housing requirements and local strategic housing market assessments (what we used to call 'housing needs studies') use a range of different methodologies and so cannot be aggregated up to a national assessment. However, referring again to the London situation where, because of the mayor's role as regional housing authority, we have more reliable data, we can note that the last assessment of housing need concluded that 48% of new homes should have at least three bedrooms; yet, the latest analysis of housing completions showed that only 27% of homes completed in 2014/15 were family-sized, with the proportion for schemes given planning consent falling to 19%. As recently as 1996/97, the proportion of new homes completed that had three or more bedrooms was 35% (Mayor of London, 2014 p 8; 2016 p 82). Research presented at a Royal Institute of British Architects (RIBA) seminar in 2008 (Bowie, 2008b) showed a clear correlation between the height of development, the density of development and the proportion of family-sized homes. The highest high-rise, hyper-dense schemes included very few, if any.

There is also increasing concern at the size of new homes. In December 2015, RIBA published a study of recently completed developer homes which concluded that, on average, new three-bedroom homes were four square metres below the government's proposed new standard (RIBA, 2015). A study in 2014 by the University of Cambridge concluded that new homes in England were, on average, 76 square metres, compared with 109 square metres in Germany and 137 square metres in Denmark (*Architects Journal*, 2014).

Some new homes, whether penthouse flats in prime central London high-rise developments or detached homes in the Home Counties, are very large but these are generally not affordable by any but the wealthiest households. While the government's recent measures to allow offices to be converted into homes without planning permission has boosted housing output, there is increasing evidence that many of these homes are very small and lacking amenities such as external play spaces for children, which are required if normal planning policies are applied.

It is also interesting to note where new homes have been built. Figure 6.1 shows the tenure of new development by type of area. While over half of new development has been in suburban areas outside London, new social and privately rented homes have been concentrated in London.

Figure 6.1: Location of development by tenure

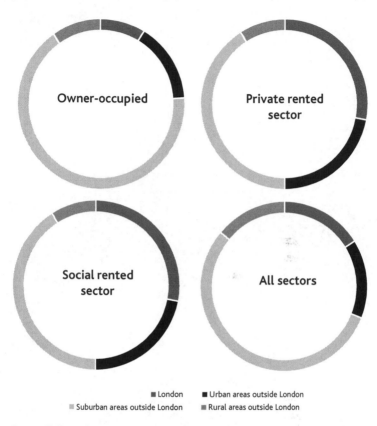

Source: EHS Housing stock report, Table 2.3 (DCLG 2016b).

7

THE INEFFICIENT USE OF THE EXISTING STOCK

Although new housing supply has fallen short on estimates of housing requirements, over the last decade, the total housing stock has increased by 7%, roughly parallel to the increase in the overall population of the UK. Yet, this increase in overall housing supply has failed to reduce the overall shortage of homes and has certainly not led to any reduction in house prices or made homes more affordable. The government's assumption that increasing supply would ease the housing crisis has proved false. Chapter Six considered the extent to which there has been a mismatch of new housing supply and the housing needs of the population. This chapter focuses on the extent to which the fact that neither the existing stock nor new housing supply are utilised effectively has contributed to the current situation. This is sometimes referred to as the 'distributionalist' argument and was the focus of Dorling's (2014) book *All that is solid*.

The total housing stock of England is currently estimated at 23.3 million dwellings. It is estimated that in 2015/16, 140,000 new homes were built, an increase on the previous year's figure of 125,000. We are therefore adding to the stock of housing at a rate of about 0.5% to 0.6% per annum. Replacing the existing stock at this rate would take 165–185 years, even if no provision was made for the growth in the household population. A total of 4.6 million homes were built before 1919 and are therefore nearly 100 years old; a further 3.9 million were built in the interwar period and are therefore more than 70 years old; only 3.5 million homes – or 15% of the stock – is less than 25 years old (EHS, 2013.4: Table 2.1 (DCLG, 2015)).

Less than 10% of property purchases relate to new properties. How we use the existing stock is therefore more critical in terms of effective use of supply and in the determination of rents and prices than how many new homes are built. We are, in fact, using the existing stock far less effectively than we have done in the past.

One issue that gets considerable attention is the number of homes that are empty. The most recent government figures estimate that there are 203,000 vacant homes in England – or about 9% of the total stock – down significantly from the 2004 figure of 319,000 (CLG live table 615 (DCLG, 2016a)). The issue of second homes is also controversial. There are some 752,000 homes in England and Wales not used as a primary residence, of which about 80,000 would appear to be third homes, rather than second homes. Of these, some 342,000 are owned by UK residents, implying that nearly half are second homes for non-UK residents. UK residents own some 362,000 second homes abroad (DCLG, 2016b). More significant, however, is the extent to which the existing housing stock is under-utilised. As Figure 7.1 shows, there has been some increase in overcrowding in recent years, predominantly in the private rented sector.

As Table 7.1 shows, 3% of households are overcrowded (including 5% of private renters and 6% of social renters but only 1% of owner-occupiers). However, the key issue is the extent of under-occupation. Table 7.1 shows that 36% of households are under-occupying, defined as having two or more rooms above the bedroom standard, while a further 34% have one spare room. Nearly 50% of owner-occupiers are categorised as under-occupying, with a further 37% having one spare room.

Figure 7.1: Overcrowded households (dwellings with more than one person per habitable room)

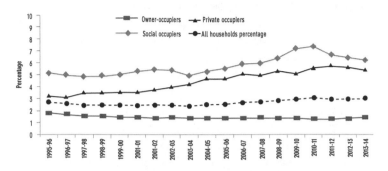

Source: English Housing Survey (2013–14 (DCLG, 2015) Table 1.14).

Table 7.1: Overcrowded and under-occupying households

All households					
	Difference from bedroom standard				
	Over-crowded	At standard	1 above standard	Under-occupied	All households
	Thousands of households				
Owner-occupiers	212	1,907	5,100	7,129	14,348
Private renters	218	1,781	1,457	603	4,059
Social renters	236	2,111	1,077	380	3,801
All tenures	**666**	**5,799**	**7,635**	**8,111**	**22,211**
	Percentages				
Owner-occupiers	1.5	13.3	35.6	19.7	100.0
Private renters	5.4	43.9	35.9	14.8	100.0
Social renters	6.2	55.5	28.3	10.0	100.0
All tenures	**3.0**	**26.1**	**34.4**	**36.5**	**100.0**

Local authorities have limited power to intervene to ensure more effective use of the existing housing stock. Councils can levy council tax on vacant homes but not apply penal rates for second homes or other under-occupied dwellings. The 'bedroom tax' can be seen as an attempt to reduce under-occupation in council homes but, as shown earlier, only 10% of social renters are under-occupying properties, and the policy was misguided in that appropriate affordable social rented homes for under-occupiers to downsize into were not available on anything like an adequate scale in most localities. Tackling the issue of under-occupied owner-occupied homes is more problematic in a context where 'the Englishman's home is his castle' and the general view is that if you have paid for a property (or at least borrowed money to pay for it), then you have the right to do with it what you want. There is, however, a broader policy issue here. One of the reasons that we need to build more homes is that the ones we already have are not always used well. It can be argued that we have enough family-sized homes already built, but that the problem is that they do not all have families living in them. If there are constraints on how many new homes we can build (whether in terms of environmental or construction resource factors), the issue of how we use existing homes gains importance.

There is a related issue in terms of the lack of local authority powers to ensure the most effective use of newly built homes. A council can require developers to build larger homes suitable for families if the need is identified in their strategic housing market assessment. However, a council has no power to ensure that once the homes are built, they are actually occupied by families, that is, that they actually meet the need for which they were intended from the council planners' perspective. Developers will sell to whoever can afford to buy the property. Use of housing in the market sector is driven by ability to pay, not by any assessment of relative need for space. There is a case for planning authorities being given a power to ensure the effective use of new homes, and to put a condition on a planning consent to ensure effective use. This is, of course, difficult to enforce as the local authority would need to monitor occupation. This is an approach being pioneered by the London borough of Islington, which, concerned that so many new flats were being bought by investors and left empty, has introduced planning conditions and fines for developers who breach the effective use condition (Islington, 2015). Where a local authority or other public sector body disposes of land for development, it is possible to impose conditions in relation to the use of the development, which could include a requirement for effective occupation and penalties for breach of covenant. Disposal covenants could also be used to control the tenure and price of completed homes, though such conditions would impact on the price paid by the developer for the land and therefore the capital receipt to the local authority or other public body.

Where planning powers cannot be used, for example, in respect of the use of existing housing, effective use may be encouraged through financial incentives. Current tax arrangements do not incentivise the most effective use of residential property. The most effective incentive would be the introduction of a high rate of council tax for under-occupying households – in effect, a 'bedroom tax' or 'surplus rooms' tax for under-occupiers. This would, in effect, be an inverse of the single person's discount operating in the current council tax regime. It is also important when considering any changes to other forms of property tax to consider whether or not measures would encourage more effective use of housing and appropriate downsizing. For example, the removal of stamp duty (or exemption for households selling a larger property to buy a smaller one) would encourage downsizing, while taxing capital gain on disposal without a downsizing exemption or discount would not. Taxing value increments for existing owner-occupiers or reintroducing 'schedule A' on imputed rental income for owner-occupiers would also act as incentives. Changes in inheritance tax in relation to the transfer of residential properties between generations would also have an impact. It does need to be acknowledged that such measures are unlikely to be popular with the under-occupying homeowner electorate, but there is a strong logic from a housing supply policy perspective. It is of little use identifying the inequity in relation to the use of existing housing stock, as Danny Dorling (2014) has done, unless you also propose reforms that will effectively tackle the problem.

8

THE FAILURE OF THE ENGLISH PLANNING SYSTEM

This chapter will first consider the planning reforms introduced by the 2010–15 Coalition government. It will then focus on three aspects of the planning system that have been central to both policy development and academic discourse since 2010. These are localism, the focus on planning for growth in relation to other sustainability criteria and the issue of development viability.

Planning reform

The Coalition government abandoned any concept of a national spatial strategy. The previous government's *Sustainable communities plan* (ODPM, 2003) identified four growth areas: the Thames Gateway, the Ashford growth area, the London/Stansted/Cambridge growth area, which was subsequently extended to Peterborough, and the South Midlands/Milton Keynes growth area. This was followed up by the designation by central government of a number of towns as growth points. The view of the Coalition government is that whether or not an area should promote residential and employment growth is a matter for local decision. The regional plans that set housing growth targets at the local authority level were withdrawn. The setting of housing targets is now a matter for individual local authorities. While London has its own regional plan, which includes 10-year housing growth targets for individual boroughs, there is no planning framework for the London metropolitan region as a whole, and the pre-existing Inter Regional Planning Forum has lapsed.

The government has sought to liberalise the planning regime and speed up the planning decision process. The *National planning policy framework* (NPPF) (DCLG, 2012) introduced a presumption in favour of development, which required local authorities to demonstrate that a development did not comply with adopted planning policy – a significant requirement when about half of the local planning authorities still did not have plans adopted under the 2004 planning regime. Local authorities who consistently missed approval timescale deadlines or lost appeals could see their planning powers taken over by central government. The permitted development rules were extended to allow developers to convert offices and industrial buildings into homes without a requirement for planning consent.

In the Localism Act 2011, the government also introduced the neighbourhood plan procedure, by which groups of residents and local businesses could develop their own statutory plan for their neighbourhood. In practice, this has weakened the ability of democratically elected local planning authorities to plan strategically, and many neighbourhood plans constrain growth.

The most significant change in national planning policy is the new focus on development viability. If a developer can demonstrate that it is not profitable for them to develop a scheme that meets the council's planning policy requirements relating to affordable housing, then they can request that these requirements are reduced or waived altogether.

Other government policy changes have had significant impacts on residential development, for example, the termination of all central government funding for new social rented housing, with the limited resources remaining being focused on the provision of rented housing that is only marginally sub-market, the misnamed 'affordable rent' programme, and some limited funding for shared-ownership homes. The government has also limited the housing benefit payable to households living in local authority, housing association and privately rented homes, reduced benefits to households considered to be under-occupying homes – the spare room subsidy or bedroom tax – and restricted the total benefit paid to a household to £500 per week. This has had a serious impact on households, especially larger families, living in higher-value areas.

The Localism Act 2011 abolished the regional planning structure and the pre-existing arrangements for sub-regional planning under the leadership of the regional assemblies, which contributed to the sub-regional strategies contained within the regional plans. In relation to the London metropolitan area, the East of England Plan had included a sub-regional strategy for the London commuter belt and for the Thames Gateway/South Essex, and the South East Plan included sub-regional strategies for the London Fringe, Kent, the Thames Gateway, the Western Corridor, Milton Keynes and Aylesbury Vale, and for the Gatwick area, all of which had a significant travel-to-work relationship with London and were part of the functional urban region.

The Localism Act requires local planning authorities to cooperate with neighbouring authorities. This is primarily a requirement for consultation through the plan preparation process. Detailed process requirements are set out in the government's NPPF and the subsequent 'National planning policy guidance' (NPPG) (DCLG, 2014b). Ministers have been keen to stress that there is no duty to agree. Nevertheless, in assessing the soundness of a local plan, a planning inspector requires the local planning authority to have met the requirement to cooperate. In a number of cases, inspectors have determined that the duty has not been. In some cases, the failure relates to a failure to consult on housing provision – either a failure to consider the implications on neighbouring authorities on under-provision within the local authority, or a failure to consult an adjacent authority as to whether the latter has housing needs that require provision in another district. The Planning Inspectorate included a schedule of such cases in its submission to the House of Commons select committee investigation into the operation of the NPPF in 2014 (House of Commons, 2014).

The government envisaged that local enterprise partnerships (LEPs) may have a role to plan in sub-regional planning. These organisations are voluntary groupings of local authorities with representatives of business but have no statutory planning powers (Bentley and Pugalis, 2013; Pugalis and Townsend, 2013). Consequently, they are not an adequately sound basis for sub-regional planning. However, local authorities do have the power to establish combined authority structures, which enable a group of local authorities to act jointly to carry out statutory functions, such as strategic planning. This has been applied in the case of local authorities in the Greater Manchester area and, more recently, in early 2016, by a group of authorities in the Liverpool city region area. Under the Planning and Compulsory Purchase Act 2004, local planning authorities can publish a joint plan for an area that incorporates parts or all of the local authorities' areas. Groups of local authorities therefore already have the power to undertake joint strategic housing market assessments and joint strategic housing land availability assessments, to agree on how housing capacity can be used across a sub-regional area, and to set housing targets for each local planning authority in a manner parallel to the process by which the mayor of London sets housing targets for the local planning authorities within London.

Localism

The Coalition government's objective in the Localism Act 2011 was to replace what they perceived as a top-down bureaucratic system of planning with a bottom-up community-led 'localist' system. Many commentators were surprised both at the speed at which the Coalition government introduced radical reforms and the extent to which 'localism', and 'the big society', became the main mantra of the Coalition's approach to governance. While there was considerable discussion as to what 'the big society' actually means, and how it is different from 'the good society' promoted by the centre-left pressure group COMPASS, there is perhaps less awareness of the basis of the ideological origins of 'localism' (see COMPASS, no date).

Part of the historiography of the concepts of the 'big society' and 'localism' lies with New Labour. In fact, the origins of the concept can be traced back to thinking within the Social Democrat Party in the early 1980s, as well as to the resistance to the growth of central government in the mid-Victorian period, epitomised in the writings of Joshua Toulmin Smith (Toulmin Smith, 1849; Bowie, 2016a).

The case for localism is perhaps set out most clearly in the Conservative Party's (2009) Green Paper *Control shift: Returning power to local communities*. The basic argument is that Britain has become one of the most centralised countries in the developed world and that the assumption that Whitehall knows best and that only uniformity can guarantee fairness is false. The Green Paper argues that technological advances have opened up a new world of power and opportunities for people and communities and that civic and social organisations should be freed up from government control. The Green Paper contends that the regional tier of government, the regional assembles, were established by central government to control local affairs. The objectives of the Conservative Party proposals were to give local communities a share in local growth, to free up local government from central control, to give people more power over local government, to give local people more ability to determine spending priorities and to remove the tier of regional government.

When the Localism Bill was published on 13 December 2010, the government press statement, under the heading 'From big government to big society' (DCLG, 2010), claimed that:

> the Big Society is what happens whenever people work together for the common good. It is about achieving our collective goals in ways that are more diverse, more local and more personal. The best contribution that central government can make is to devolve power, money and knowledge to those best placed to find the best solutions to local needs: elected local representatives, frontline public service professionals, social enterprises, charities, co-ops, community groups, neighbourhoods and individuals.

Local government in England has been weak in terms of both financial and legal autonomy when compared with structures in most Western

European countries, while regional government has been neither democratically accountable nor resourced, and, beyond London, is now deceased. Under Blair and Brown, New Labour did not reverse the centralisation tendencies of Thatcher and Major, and the combination of privatisation and increased central control led to a disempowerment of local governance structures and a demoralisation of local politicians – the centralisation of power within the Labour Party was a critical part of this process.

So, policies that would empower local government and reinvigorate local political activity should be welcomed. However, the government's localism agenda and specifically the proposals in the Localism Bill will not have that effect – or at least not in a way that libertarian socialists would find positive – for despite the rhetoric, local authorities have not been empowered. Grant support from central government is being reduced, while councils' ability to raise taxation or private finance is not, in fact, being increased. While national standards and regulations are being weakened and local authorities are being given more powers to determine their own policies, notably in relation to housing and planning, with reductions in central government support leading to severe cuts in services and public sector staffing, councils who want to use these freedoms are restricted in their capacity to be proactive where new policies require significant expenditure. So, while authorities in better-off areas who have significant land and property assets may be empowered, in practice, those in less well-off areas, who will generally have fewer resources, will not actually be able to fund the service improvements and housing and education infrastructure that they need. Therefore, in pratice, central government has quite cleverly transferred responsibility to local authorities while reducing their ability to carry out their responsibilities.

However, the real issue of localism is the bypassing of democratically elected local government structures to empower neighbourhoods. The fundamental proposal within the planning clauses in the Localism Act is that groups of residents will be able to set up neighbourhood forums to write the plans for their neighbourhood, which would then be put to a neighbourhood ballot. Residents of a neighbourhood would also be able to determine whether individual developments could proceed. This may appear initially attractive until it is understood that there will be few rules for this new framework. First, any three residents can set up a neighbourhood forum. While this is supposed to be open to all residents who want to live in any area, there will be no regulation by local authorities or other bodies to ensure that the forums operate in an inclusive way. There has been a suggestion that local councillors might be members, but there is no proposal that neighbourhood forum officers in urban areas should be subject to election and re-election – in rural areas, the existing parish council becomes the neighbourhood planning authority.

Localism has its attractions. The difficulty is that most local neighbourhood planning activity has been oppositionist – existing residents protecting their area from developments or people who may devalue their area and their properties. The Localism Bill is therefore a charter for NIMBYs – people who oppose development 'in my backyard'. Moreover, power without resources is a charter for people who want to stop development rather than those who want –or need – to see things happen. The house-builders, not surprisingly, are concerned as to how any homes at all are going to be built. What we are likely to see is the bigger developers, the house-builders and the retail developers such as Tescos and Sainsburys, not only funding the plan-making process, but also then making payments to individual households in exchange for their support for a development. Tory ministers have referred to this as 'enlightened self-interest' but I do not see anything enlightened here. The idea may be based on 'nudge' theory, but it can also be seen as a form of bribery. Is this the best way to get the development that our growing population needs in the right places? Surely we need some kind of democratically accountable planning system to ensure that development is sustainable in economic, social and environmental terms, to mediate between conflicting interests, and to protect the interests of residents and neighbourhoods that are not self-sustaining and self-financing.

Without such intermediaries, there is a risk that localism leads to self-contained ghettoes of the rich and self-contained ghettoes of the poor. As libertarian socialists, our challenge is to get the right balance between neighbourhood self-determination and equalising access to resources – wealth, income, power and fixed resources (good-quality homes, good schools, good health facilities, decent leisure facilities and good public transport), which are not spatially distributed equally. This libertarianism of the free market and letting the better-off do what they want under the populist notion of 'localism' has to be challenged. Progressives need to think twice before standing up and saying how much they welcome localism. Of course, there are new opportunities to promote local socialised or even socialist plans, but we also need strategic planning and a fairer national system of wealth, income and resource redistribution.

Planning for growth

A central focus of the approach to planning of the Coalition government of 2010–15 was that planning should enable economic growth rather than obstruct it. It became increasingly clear that planning policy was driven by the Treasury and by the Prime Minister's office, rather than by the Department of Communities and Local Government. This shift can be seen as having its origins in the Blair and Brown governments. Kate Barker, economist and member of the Monetary Policy Committee, undertook a review of housing supply in 2004 and then of planning in 2006. The *Plan for growth* statement of 23 March 2011 was published by the Chancellor of the Exchequer (HM Treasury, 2011). When the NPPF was published in March 2012, it was clear that economic growth was to be prioritised over environmental and social sustainability. While the National Trust and the Council for the Protection of Rural England (CPRE) ran a campaign to protect environmental sustainability principles, seeking to defend the green belt and to stop what was seen as a threat to the countryside, there was little debate over the fact that giving preference to economic growth objectives, which the government incorrectly equated with economic sustainability, might have negative impacts on social sustainability objectives. Representations to include in the statement of planning objectives a phrase such as 'and seek to reduce spatial inequity and social polarisation' were disregarded (Highbury Group on Housing Delivery, 2011). The NPPF established a presumption in favour of 'sustainable development' but did not provide a definition of sustainable development that was sufficiently specific to allow local planning authorities to apply clear criteria for assessing economic, environmental and social sustainability to individual development proposals.

The requirement in the NPPF that both local planning policy and individual developments should allow for 'competitive returns to a willing landowner and willing developer' made the government's priorities explicit. It also made it clear that local planning authorities should not expect private sector developments to provide subsidy towards local authorities' own transport and social infrastructure priorities where this might have a negative impact on landowners' and developers' profit margins. The impact on this increased focus on development viability as seen from the developer's perspective is discussed in the next section.

Development viability

The requirement that plans demonstrate deliverability has given additional importance to the issue of viability appraisal. However, there is also a requirement that plans should be soundly based on evidence of need and demand. In a context of limited resources, there is therefore a potential conflict between setting policies and targets that are based on evidence of need and demand, and setting policies and targets that are demonstrably deliverable. One of the key purposes of planning is to assess the extent of such conflicts.

However, the issue of how to respond to such a conflict is more problematic. One approach is to respond to a negative viability assessment by constraining policies and targets to what is deliverable. However, an alternative is to assess different mechanisms, including funding mechanisms, to achieve the delivery of needs-based targets. This is one of the central purposes of an implementation plan.

Any viability assessment needs to have regard to the availability of both public and private funding. There is a risk that in the current context of public funding constraints and uncertainty as to the ability of a volatile private market to fund plan implementation, targets will be set significantly below those identified from a needs-based approach. To take one example, the fact that public funds are no longer available for social rented housing may be used to justify a zero target even where a strategic housing market assessment demonstrates a significant need. The current emphasis in the NPPF on planning policy requirements that make schemes non-viable not being imposed could be used to justify this position.

There is a separate requirement in legislation and the Community Infrastructure Levy (CIL) regulations that local authority proposals for CIL need to be tested for viability in terms of not making development as a whole across a planning area non-viable. A local planning authority is required to assess the potential impact on pipeline schemes of a proposed CIL levy. While such assessments have been used to support CIL proposals, it could be argued that the assessment by inspectors has not been very rigorous.

Once a borough-wide target is set, a financial assessment should be part of a process for assessing the potential for applying the target to an individual scheme if (and only if) there is a proposed departure from policy. This assessment can then relate to the specific costs and values of a known development proposal based on the facts available at a specific point in time. An assessment can model different development options and scenarios for different costs and values over a development period. It should be noted that the London Plan, as adopted in 2004 and as amended in 2008, 2011 and 2015, separates the scheme assessment from the overall target-setting process. This was intentional as the draft plan in 2002 had originally proposed differential borough affordable housing targets based on borough-level modelling of development viability. These were removed in favour of a London-wide target related primarily to an assessment of need and development capacity. There was a concern that to base borough targets solely on a viability assessment at a fixed point in time would prejudice a local planning authority's ability to negotiate a higher proportion where this was justified by an appraisal of a specific development proposal. This was in recognition that costs and values could vary widely between different schemes within a local planning authority area, and would also vary over time depending on a range of external factors.

The land market does not operate independently of planning policy. In fact, planning policy requirements, such as a requirement for affordable housing, a density policy or a requirement to contribute from development value to transport and social infrastructure, may constrain the value of land. Any developer should have regard to these constraints before committing to acquiring a development site. Any relaxation in density constraints will enhance residential land value, as would any removal of or reduction in an affordable housing target or requirement for planning contributions. Any tightening of policies could reduce residential land value, with the potential consequence of either increasing developer profit or reducing sale prices – or potentially a combination of the two.

In areas where most residential development is on brownfield land, the use value of a potential residential site in its pre-existing use (assuming that this can be operationalised) or an alternative use for which planning consent may be granted is a critical factor in determining the relative profitability of residential use. Financial appraisals of residential sites on brownfield land must therefore have regard to existing or alternative uses. In viability assessments at the development plan level, it is evidentially better to base assessments on the market values for land, adjusted to take account of emerging policies that have yet to be fully reflected in the market.

Any financial appraisal needs to have regard to the level of return to both landowner and developer, both to bring the site onto the development market and to attract private investment into the development (where this is necessary). The NPPF, which refers to a willing landowner and willing developer being able to achieve competitive returns, implies that it is primarily for the landowner and developer to determine the return that they are seeking and that it is not the role of a public body to question such assumptions – a position, to a certain extent, supported by the Royal Institute of Chartered Surveyors (RICS, 2012) guidance. While financial appraisal toolkits generally have a baseline assumption as to a reasonable rate of return for a developer (and also for a building contractor who is not taking any speculative risk), there is no guidance on a reasonable value uplift for a landowner in relation to existing use. Previous Homes and Communities Agency (HCA)-endorsed guidance in relation to a 20% norm was withdrawn. It is essential that this guidance is reviewed. It is recognised that this will vary from site to site – clearly, a 20% uplift on a site with an Existing Use Value (EUV) of £200 million a hectare is a different order of profit from a 20% uplift on a site with an EUV of £20,000 a hectare – but any guidance that does not deal with this issue is of limited use to both local planning authorities and potential public funding bodies such as the HCA, the mayor and local authorities who are seeking to ensure the most cost-effective use of development capacity and public funding. There is, of course, the risk that a development site may be frozen where agreement cannot be reached. Where landowners are unwilling to proceed with development on the terms acceptable to the local planning authority, the local planning authority does have the power to seek to compulsorily acquire land, in which case, there is a process for determining the compensation value.

As the planning status of land clearly has an impact on its value, local planning authorities, in making land allocations within local plans, often allocate land as mixed use without being specific about residential components and without a detailed brief. Mixed-use allocations often have the consequence that a developer brings forward a project that is most profitable for them. The more specific the brief, the greater the constraint imposed on development options and therefore on the land value. A local planning authority could, however, make a specific land-use allocation for affordable housing, or specify the proportion of a site to be used for affordable housing. Any such allocation or planning brief would need to be specific as to the form of affordable housing sought in terms of type, mix, tenure and affordability.

There is a greater potential for local planning authorities to compulsorily acquire potential residential development sites. This is most usefully applied to greenfield sites or other sites with low value (eg vacant or underused industrial sites) where the site is appropriate for residential development but where no residential zoning has been as yet declared. Where a site has been allocated for residential development but no scheme has been brought forward, the local authority could 'auction' their ability to Compulsory Purchase (CPO) the site to the best bidder – based on a judgement as to which bidder is most able to comply with policy requirements in relation to affordable housing mix and tenure, space requirements, and design standards. The possibility of the purchase price being based on the valuation at designation needs to be considered as this would avoid landowners benefiting from land value inflation relating to any subsequent period – in essence, avoiding any benefit to the developer arising from delay in bringing a scheme forward for development.

A development model that relies on private development value to provide affordable housing as well as social infrastructure, such as education, health and leisure facilities, and transport and utilities infrastructure, is no longer viable. The government needs to establish a model for funding affordable housing that does not require a provider to either sell market homes or dispose of existing assets. While it is not necessary for the government to provide 100% grant for social housing, the best option would be to return to the mixed funding regime that operated between 1988 and about 2000, before competitive bidding was introduced. The cost of each scheme should be assessed against a benchmark, which considers land acquisition costs and build costs, and the ability to raise private finance from the capitalisation of the rental should be assessed. For a mixed-tenure and or mixed-use development, the ability of the private development to cross-subsidise affordable housing provision should be assessed but not assumed. Except in the case of highly profitable residential schemes on premium sites, transport and social infrastructure should be funded separately – generally from taxation.

Affordable housing outputs should be determined by an assessment of requirements, rather than by the economics of a specific development, and grants should be made available to meet the scheme deficit assessed through a financial appraisal. No assumption should be made about a developer or housing association being able to cross-subsidise a specific development from its own resources. This will mean that for most schemes, a much higher level of government subsidy is required than under the funding model operated under the last few years, and as shown by the earlier appraisals, this subsidy requirement will vary widely between schemes.

SECTION THREE
THERE IS AN ALTERNATIVE

9
A RADICAL PROGRAMME FOR REFORM

This concluding section starts with a discussion on some key policy issues. It will then seek to establish principles for a new housing policy and planning policy relating to housing supply before setting out a specific reform programme.

Forms of investment: bricks or benefits?

This is a critical issue for any government to consider – whether subsidies to provide affordable housing should be in the form of investment in the provision of new homes so that they can be let at relatively low rents – bricks and mortar subsidy – or whether subsidies should be in the form of revenue payments to households to rent market homes that would otherwise be unaffordable at their prevailing levels of income. It is now logical for a government to again provide significant investment subsidies rather than rely on revenue subsidies because the government can set the terms on which grant-funded property is occupied, including ensuring continuing occupation by households in housing need, and can ensure that such homes are available for future generations. As the value of a property increases, it becomes a public asset against which further borrowing can be raised. The case for a rebalancing of investment subsidies and revenue subsidies has been set out in two recent reports – SHELTER's (2012) *Bricks or benefits?* and the Institute for Public Policy Research's (IPPR's) *Together at home* (Hull, 2012). A huge advantage of subsidising the (publicly owned) bricks would be that the subsidy does not leak away as a de facto subsidy to landlords, which is the effective role of housing benefit and housing allowance payments. A significant increase in the supply of social rented housing could help to reduce rent inflation in the private rented sector.

Socialising the private rented sector

While we have increasingly privatised the social housing sector, we have failed to socialise the private rented sector. The private rented sector is, in effect, deregulated. There are no rent controls and no minimum security of tenure, and statutory regulation of minimum standards is limited to houses in multiple occupation, and, in practice, largely ineffective. Yet, with the homeownership sector shrinking and social housing stock continuing to decline, the private rented sector is booming, with the bottom end of the sector fuelled by housing benefit. Yet, attempts to cap local housing allowance payments to private tenants, while disadvantaging lower-income households, have not, as yet, brought private rents down in the way that the government had hoped. In London, the average private rent represents 41% of an average household's income; in some London boroughs, the proportion is over 50%. In less expensive areas of England, the proportion can be much lower, at 10–25%. There is a strong case for socialising at least part of the private rented sector. Given the shortage of social housing, the private rented sector needs to provide accommodation not just for short-term singles and couples, but also for medium- and longer-term accommodation for family households. There is therefore a case for introducing a voluntary regulation system where landlords will guarantee a minimum level of security of tenure, a fixed level of rent and service charges, and physical and management standards in exchange for the direct payment of housing benefit and grants, where necessary, for improvements. Where the regulation is ineffective, there is a case for transferring ownership into the public sector or to some other form of 'socialised' ownership. One option would be a strengthening of the existing provisions for housing management orders, where a local authority can take over the management of a badly managed privately rented property without having to pay for the acquisition of the property.

Homeownership is not always the solution

The starting point for any new strategy is to recognise that even though the majority of households may aspire to homeownership, it is not a feasible option for an increasing proportion of households. The government cannot control house price inflation and there is no guarantee that a significant increase in supply would depress house prices sufficiently to make homeownership accessible to a significantly higher proportion of households – at least in the South of England, where housing demand is most acute. To provide grants to middle-income homeowners, to reduce stamp duty or to provide more shared-ownership or mortgage guarantee arrangements is both expensive for the government and generally ineffective as these initiatives just boost house price inflation further. Assistance to one group just disadvantages other groups, as the key worker housing initiative demonstrated, with nurses and police officers leapfrogging bus drivers in the climb up the homeownership ladder.

Rebalancing the relationship between the public and the private sector

The private sector has a role. However, the private market should not be the driver of housing policy and housing development. Moreover, the recession has shown us the need for government intervention, both to counteract the impact of market failure and to effectively regulate the market to reduce the likelihood of market failure occurring. However, we must remind ourselves that the market in a boom period does not provide the homes we need either. There is therefore a need to rebalance the relationship between the public and private sectors – for boom periods as well as recessions. The market is based on the profit motive and has a short- and medium-term focus. Public policy has to focus on the long term and the needs of future generations, as well as the needs of the present. Moreover, it is only the public sector that can consider economic, social and environmental perspectives. Furthermore, it is only the public sector, whether working at national, regional or local levels, or in a county, district or neighbourhood, which operates within a democratically accountable structure.

Where the public sector shares risk, the public sector should also take a share in any profit or value appreciation. It is the public sector that, after full consideration of the available evidence, must set out priorities for the type of housing to be provided and determine through its planning powers the appropriate locations for sustainable developments that link to employment opportunities, transport networks and social infrastructure, such as schools and health and leisure facilities. It is the public sector that should coordinate the acquisition and development of land. It is the public sector that should set the parameters for access to different types of housing. Private finance can make a contribution to funding new development, as it did in the case of the former Housing Corporation's mixed-finance programme, but private finance can only be a supplement to public investment and not a substitute for it.

Resources and powers

It is critical that the government, whether operating at the national, regional or local level, has sufficient resources in terms of land and funding to invest in the homes we need and to meet both quantitative and qualitative targets. Discussions on the extent of the public sector deficit and resource constraints in this so-called period of austerity often fail to recognise that such constraints are largely a matter of political choice. A government can choose to increase the resources available to it by raising further income from changes to tax regimes, for example, through a more progressive income tax system, modifying capital gains and inheritance tax, modifying council tax, or introducing a new property tax.

The government can also divert expenditure from one programme to another, for example, from nuclear submarine replacement to housing investment. The argument for dealing with squalor within our own country before seeking to maintain and expand our imperial role is not a new one (see, eg, Masterman, 1902, 1907). However, the public sector, especially local authorities, also need new powers to ensure that resources are not wasted: powers to acquire land for housing development at existing use value so that speculators do not take all the gain from value appreciation; powers to ensure the effective occupation of privately developed homes; and powers to ensure that utilities companies and other private and semi-privatised organisations provide the infrastructure to support new residential development.

Localism and spatial justice

Localism will not deliver social justice. A governance structure that gives the freedom to local councils to decide whether or not to allow the building of new homes needs a set of checks and balances. A governance structure that transfers this decision-making power to self-elected unaccountable neighbourhood forums carries with it even more dangers. The temptation for neighbourhoods, which are well-off, to protect their own leafy areas from new development and to protect their own property values is irresistible. For poorer neighbourhoods that need investment in their homes, the power to make a plan is of little use if it is not supported by resources beyond those that they can themselves generate. The proposals for neighbourhood planning do not recognise the differential power of different neighbourhoods, or the fact that planning is a conflict between conflicting interests, and planners should not just be looking to the greatest good and widest public benefit, but be seeking to mitigate social polarisation and spatial injustice.

All plans at whatever level need to be the subject of impact assessment as to who gains and who loses out, not just within a community, but in terms of the wider impacts on people outside the neighbourhood. Planners and politicians need to consider the opportunity costs of not developing – what opportunities are missed? Planners and politicians need to be reminded that there is a social agenda to planning as well as the environmental and economic agendas. If we are to avoid further social polarisation and achieve genuine mixed communities, we need to provide genuinely affordable homes in areas that are mainly owner-occupied. This may not always be popular with existing residents. We cannot rely on the altruism of the well-housed middle classes, just as we cannot rely on the philanthropy of the millionaires and billionaires. We need government intervention and funding to both protect the most disadvantaged in existing communities and to provide for future generations. Too many politicians on the Left have swallowed the localism mantra. Of course, resident engagement in planning and housing is important but it is not a panacea and it is not a sufficient mantra to justify the abrogation of the responsibilities of elected politicians.

The need for a new strategic approach

An aggregate of local initiatives will not deliver the homes we need. Current provision is only a third of what is needed. In London alone, we need to add 50% to the existing housing stock over the next 30 years. It is not acceptable for any national government to be neutral on the key issue of where people will live, work and play in the future. Growth is not solely a matter for the local district council or neighbourhood forum. Incentives for local communities are not enough – the application of nudge theory is not a solution. Governments at national and regional level, where it still exists, have a shared responsibility for deciding where homes should go and for funding the infrastructure to support new communities.

We need a national spatial plan, and we need regional and sub-regional planning back. We need to recognise that there needs to be some spatial redistribution of investment – just following a volatile market does not constitute a strategy. Ministers of housing, planning and local government have a responsibility beyond just saying 'it's all up to you folks'. The government also has a role in ensuring that we have a construction sector that is fit to deliver, that we have a sufficiently skilled workforce and that we have the materials we need and the efficient supply chains. If materials and skills are in short supply, the government needs to direct them to the most urgent needs – in this context, this is social housing not upmarket luxury housing for the millionaires and the billionaires. The government has done this before in previous periods of austerity and crisis. While it can be questioned whether this really is an age of austerity, in the sense that limiting government income and then limiting government expenditure is a matter of political choice, from a housing perspective, there is certainly a crisis in terms of shortage that is equivalent to, if not more serious than, the reconstruction periods after the First and Second World Wars.

The basic principles for a new housing strategy

It is important to return to the core principles for a new progressive housing policy. This is necessary if we are to overcome the legacy of decades of half-baked and ill-thought-out ad hoc initiatives. I would suggest the following:

- The state should not promote one specific tenure over another.
- While recognising household aspirations, housing policy and programmes should seek to meet the differing needs of the full range of households, and focus support on those households who need assistance to access housing that is secure and of good quality and are unable to access appropriate homes in the market sector.
- Government subsidies should be focused on investment for longer-term public benefit rather than on supporting the consumption of housing by individual households.
- Government subsidies should not be used to support capital appreciation by individual households. Any public investment in private provision must be based on equity retention by a public sector body, with a share in value appreciation being used for wider public benefit.

- As housing is in short supply relative to demand, there is a need to disincentivise the underuse of the existing housing stock, irrespective of whether the housing is in public or private ownership.

A number of policy priorities follow from the application of these principles to the current UK context. In setting out the following reform proposals, it should be noted that housing and planning are devolved powers in Scotland, Wales and Northern Ireland. Both context and legislation are different for each nation. The propositions set out here relate mainly to England, though some aspects will also apply in the other nations within the UK:

- In most parts of England, given the relationship between costs and household incomes, the provision of housing for lower- and some middle-income households will require some form of public subsidy. Subsidies for investment in provision on the basis of social rented housing by a public body or other non-profit-making body ensures that access to housing is on the basis of assessed relative need and remains available for use by such households in perpetuity.
- Collectively owned housing assets part-funded through the state (ie by taxpayers) should not be disposed of so long as there remains a household unable to access market housing for whom the asset is suitable.
- There needs to be a government programme for funding the regeneration and replacement of council estates that are no longer of an acceptable standard, which is not dependent on raising private finance, increasing rents or cross-subsidies from private development. Estate regeneration should be based on the principle of no loss of affordable housing supply, unless there is an identified surplus.
- Rents for social rented housing (local authority and housing association) should be at a level affordable by households in low-income employment without the need for support through housing benefit. Applying a benchmark that no household should pay more than 30% of net household income in housing costs is a reasonable starting point. Social rented housing should have security of tenure.

This is critical for low-income households, who will often have little other stability in their lives in terms of lacking secure employment.

- Financial support should only be given for private rented provision where housing is of good quality, secure, affordable and accessed on the basis of a housing need assessment. An element of the private rented sector should be regulated and subject to rent control. Private landlords should be encouraged to opt into a regulatory system that guarantees the direct payment of housing benefit on the condition that properties meet a qualitative physical standard, that tenancies are a minimum of five years and that management is subject to regulation. This will create a stable and affordable component of the private rented sector and could supplement social housing provision.

- There should be no subsidies, including tax incentives or allowances, in relation to homeownership. Individual homeowning households, as well as landlords, should be taxed on the value appreciation of properties owned, either on an annual basis or on disposal. Council tax bandings need to be expanded to ensure a higher rate of tax for owners of the most valuable properties. This tax income should then be used to support investment in housing for lower-income households. There is a strong case for replacing stamp duty (as a tax on purchase) by property taxes that relate to value appreciation.

- The owners of vacant land and property should be subject to higher rates of taxation. Householders who under-occupy dwellings should be subject to higher rates of taxation, with the tax income generated then used to support investment for lower-income households. This could be achieved through amendments to council tax. There also needs to be the removal of the current arrangements for the preferential tax treatment of international, 'non-dom' and corporate purchasers of residential property. In a context of a housing shortage, it is unacceptable that a significant proportion of new residential development is not contributing effectively to meeting housing needs.

- It is unacceptable that inheritance is now the main source of funds for households to enter homeownership in higher-value areas. There needs to be a higher rate of taxation on the transfer of property assets between generations.

- Local authorities need to be empowered to acquire development land at close to existing use value so that speculation in land is minimised and the costs of providing new homes is significantly reduced.

- Local planning authorities need to be explicit as to the public policy priorities for the use of development sites, and have the power to reject development proposals that do not meet these public policy objectives.

- Except where a surplus is identified, new development should focus on the provision of family-sized homes that are affordable by lower- and middle-income households, that are at low and medium densities, and that have access to employment opportunities, public transport, schools, health facilities, leisure opportunities and quality open space. This may mean the consideration of urban extension as well as small-scale suburban intensification. This does mean that we need more space. However, we can provide decent affordable homes without concreting over the countryside. New settlements must meet environmental, economic and social sustainability objectives. In the past, we have created new slums to replace old slums. We cannot make this mistake again. We certainly want to avoid continuing the recent trend of building higher and higher. This is neither cost-effective nor socially sustainable.

Some basic principles for a new approach to planning for housing supply

The main purpose of a national spatial planning framework should be to guide the spatial distribution of development by allocating investment resources from national budgets to support sustainable development in the identified areas. A national planning framework is essential in order to ensure that development is focused on locations where environmental, economic and social sustainability objectives can be achieved. A national spatial framework also needs to address spatial inequalities in terms of supporting the generation of a more balanced economy and to ensure access to jobs, housing and amenities in areas of the country that are in deficit. A national framework is necessary to provide a framework at sub-national level, whether this be on a regional, city-region or sub-regional basis.

With the Planning and Compulsory Purchase Act 2004, sub-national strategic planning moved from a county basis to a regional basis, with the abolition of the county-led structure plans and the introduction of regional spatial strategies (the framework for regional spatial planning having already been reintroduced for London under the Greater London Authority Act 1999 and the requirement for a spatial development strategy for London). Outside London, regional strategies included sub-regional components whose preparation involved county councils, district councils and unitary councils, but components that derived their authority from being part of approved regional spatial strategies. With the abolition of regional spatial strategies, these sub-regional components also become invalid, unless adopted and incorporated into local development frameworks by the district and unitary councils concerned. However, at present, this is not possible for the majority of local planning authorities, who have not, as yet, adopted core strategies under the 2004 Act framework. In some metropolitan areas, such as Manchester and Leeds, with Birmingham and Sheffield following, there has been some move towards collaboration between district authorities at a city-region level. However, at present, there is no statutory framework for plan-making on a cross-authority basis, though there is provision under the 2004 Act for authorities to adopt joint local development documents covering areas within more than one local planning authority.

While the current government's proposals envisage cooperation on spatial planning between neighbouring authorities, and propose a duty to collaborate, at present, it is unclear whether this duty will amount to preparing a common spatial plan. Responsibility for developing infrastructure plans is unclear, though it is perceived that there may be a role for county councils, as well as district and unitary councils, as local planning authorities. The Coalition government appeared to be supportive of a two-tier county–district structure and have opposed the establishment of any more unitary authorities.

It is important to identify the reasons why a planning system that is driven solely by the perspective of a single local planning authority is problematic. The first and most critical point to make is that local planning authorities are not equal. Some areas are better off than others both in terms of the wealth and income of their residents and in terms of access to services. Some areas may have difficulty identifying appropriate sites to provide development to meet the needs of their existing and future residents; other areas may have significant development capacity. This is recognised in the New Labour government's identification first of growth areas and then of growth points. To take an example, the Thames Gateway was identified as having a capacity to provide homes, jobs and services beyond the needs of the existing residents of the area, which could contribute to relieving the pressure on other areas in the greater South East. The eco-towns were seen as fulfilling a similar function, if on a smaller scale. The Coalition government now sees these development proposals as having to first satisfy existing local residents, rather than meet a wider objective.

Second, employment and housing market areas do not coincide with local district boundaries. Most employment catchment areas operate on a city-regional principle, with a significant number of workers within a city commuting in from adjacent suburban, semi-rural and rural districts. The previous government advised local planning authorities to collaborate on a city-regional or sub-regional basis.

Third, the provision of major new transport and social infrastructure, as well as retail, commercial, industrial, leisure and residential development, may have impacts beyond a single local planning authority area. The definition of a strategic development set out in the strategic planning guidance for London (GOL circular 1/2008, see GOL 2008) could be applied in other parts of England. The pre-existing planning guidance, both in terms of Planning Policy Statement (PPS) 11 and PPS12, recognised that significant local development decisions need to have regard to the spatial context. Guidance on planning policies for housing in PPS3 is explicit that assessments of housing demand and capacity need to be undertaken on a regional or sub-regional basis.

However, the *Open source planning* Green Paper (Conservative Party, 2010a) went beyond the notion that planning decisions should be devolved from national and regional levels to a local planning authority level. The proposals are based on the principle of double devolution and advocate neighbourhood planning as a basis for plan-making. The principle is that the existing residents of a specific neighbourhood are best placed to plan their own future. The Coalition government seem to wish to apply this principle both to plan-making – district-level plans should be an aggregation of neighbourhood-based plans – and to development control – local residents should decide which development schemes are given consent.

This focus on localism has put some planning organisations in a dilemma. The new focus has been welcomed by many local councillors and councils who opposed targets being imposed on them by central government or regional bodies. Some planning organisations also take the view that planning has been too centralist. There is also a view that public participation has been weak, and that the Coalition's case for greater public involvement in both plan-making and the planning decision process has some validity. It is true that both regional-level planning and, in some cases, the preparation of core strategies have had little active engagement from the 'general public', with the consultation process only engaging existing organised interest groups. Regional spatial strategy examinations in public (EiPs) have generally had relatively limited attendance, and that limited attendance has mainly consisted of 'professional consultees'. It is true that a more local focus, whether neighbourhood-based or scheme-specific, is more likely to generate public interest as the impact on residents or neighbours of a specific development proposal is more obvious. Part of the difficulty with local plan-making processes is that with local planning authorities focusing on district-wide documents such as the statements of community involvement, initial options and preferred options reports, and then core strategies, as well as attempts to influence

Regional Spatial Strategies (RSSs) and sub-regional strategies, there has been little time to focus on neighbourhood plans, whether for growth points, for existing residential communities or for site development briefs. In fact, the majority of development briefs, even those drawn up for councils rather than on behalf of developers, are prepared by private consultancies – the council is in a reactive rather than proactive role, and local council officials and councillors may not be seen as leading the process. Consequently, the democratic accountability of the plan-making process may not be explicit.

However, neighbourhood planning, whether in the form of area masterplans, site development briefs or the consultation process on major planning applications, is important. These processes cannot be self-contained, however, and must be set within a wider policy context. The planning of a neighbourhood must have regard to potential future needs rather than just the preferences of existing residents. Moreover, it must have regard to wider impacts. Planning is about allocating a scarce resource – in terms of space – to a specific land use or uses. Planning decisions have negative as well as positive impacts. Planning decisions are a balance between interests that are often in conflict. As the Royal Town Planning Institute (RTPI) states, planning is not just about place-making, it is also about the mediation of space. Planning decisions involve making choices, and as these involve subjective judgements, the process is inherently political and therefore has to be accountable to the democratic governance structure.

Planning is not just about conserving the past; it is also about planning for the future. Neighbourhood planning must therefore be more than just defending the existing heritage and built form. It also has to deal with demands arising from population growth and change. It also has to at least try to mitigate spatial social inequalities in terms of access to resources and facilities. This means that plan-making has to be more than a statement of vision. Allocation of land uses to meet the vision is an important component of plan-making.

However, a plan that cannot be implemented is not a very useful plan. The issue of implementation is critical and a largely under-recognised part of the planning process. Every plan needs to be accompanied by an implementation plan, and every planning application by a development appraisal. The planning profession is only discredited by propounding visions that have no chance of getting beyond the visionary stage. Residents lose faith in a process that lacks realism.

Planning is therefore a complex balancing act:

- between different objectives that may be in conflict;
- between planning for the needs of the present and the needs of the future;
- between the interests of individuals and the broader (often unrepresented) public; and
- between what is an ideal outcome and what is deliverable.

While it is important that planners have 'vision', it is also important to recognise that different individuals and communities have their own visions. There is no professional expertise that justifies a planner's vision as necessarily being the best vision. Planners are not technocratic gods.

For some, 'localism' has become a panacea. After more than 30 years during which the public sector has been seen as bad and the private sector as good, the new mantra is 'centralism bad and localism good'. For some, this has become 'planning bad, neighbourhood self-determination good'. This fails to recognise that even 'neighbourhood' is not easily defined, and fails to ask: who are the residents who are determining their future? Who determines how neighbourhoods make their own decisions unless there are accountable structures – and what types of decisions can be made at a local neighbourhood level? Or, does 'localism' in its purest form mean that within a neighbourhood, residents are not subject to any external constraints?

If there is to be a rebalancing of decision-making powers between different tiers of government, not just in relation to land-use planning and development matters, but on matters of service provision and management (such as schools and health services) or resource allocation matters (eg taxation and grant-making), there needs to be both clarity on the process and an assessment of the potential impacts. A difficulty with Coalition government devolution initiative was that there was a confusion between devolving decision-making to a more local level of governance, for example, to parish or ward councils, and the proposal for residents to be more involved in the decision-making process. The two were and are not synonymous, and any proposals to pass decision-making from locally accountable bodies to 'resident groups' or to individuals are problematic in terms of ensuring that such groups or individuals are representative and are not solely exercising powers in a way that is primarily for their own benefit. The proposal that schemes with resident support should be taken out of the statutory planning decision-making process under the Neighbourhood Development Order provisions of the Localism Act 2011 was an example of a proposition that may be popular but problematic where it is not accompanied by clear mechanisms for implementation and resolving those details of ensuring public benefit and avoiding corruption and personal gain that the statutory process was established to deal with.

Therefore, localism has to be responsible. Whereas there are elements of the pre-existing planning system that can be seen as too centralist and insufficiently engaging local residents in the planning process, there is a risk that unconstrained localism will actually generate policy decisions that are only of benefit to a minority of residents, and that will, in fact, increase rather than reduce spatial inequity, in other words, that will lead to benefits for the informed professional class at the expense of everybody else – benefits for the better-off neighbourhoods at the expense of other areas. Responsible localism has to move beyond immediate neighbourhood self-interest. The most successful civic leaders are those that have led development and transformation to meet long-term challenges – economic, environmental and social, rather than focused solely on conservation and heritage. Planning is a fundamental component of dynamic civic leadership. The term 'civic' is important as it combines three components:

- a sense of place;
- a sense of accountability; and
- a sense of the public interest and purpose.

The term 'dynamic' is equally important as it reflects the fact that planning is about adaptation – adapting to external factors. There are short-term plans, medium-term plans and long-term plans. There is an interaction between plan-making, plan implementation and plan revision. A plan is not some document that is a fixed masterplan for an indefinite period. The future can be projected – it cannot be predicted. Monitoring and updating the evidence base are essential components of a dynamic plan-making process.

The challenge remains how to adapt the planning structures and processes to reflect the localism agenda while retaining a planning regime and practice that has regard to what are loosely called 'externalities', both factors that impact on a neighbourhood and the deliverability of its own self-determined plans, and externalities in terms of the impact that decisions within a neighbourhood have on the world beyond the neighbourhood. The fundamental issue is to how to establish new decision-making structures and appraisal systems that deal with the different interests referred to earlier. Both plan-making and the planning application decision-making system have become too focused on process rather than output and impact analysis. As planning authorities at various levels, national, regional and local, have produced extensive policy requirements and guidance, both plan-making and application determination have been predicated on checking policy compliance. Even sustainability appraisals, by moving to checklist systems, have led to a loss of focus, especially with the appraisal systems becoming a specialist industry. The planning process has become too much of a ritual process between different sets of consultants, with an increasing dependence on specialist expertise, a ritual that becomes even less transparent as the public sector increasingly depends on just those private consultants who are representing their developer clients. Given that most applications are not policy-compliant in all areas – not surprisingly given that policy requirements are so extensive – a planning decision report will often present a decision or recommendation 'made on balance' without explicitly assessing the issues of non-compliance. Even when decisions are taken at member level, the full policy assessment may be missing as councillors may actually raise points outside the formal policy position of the planning authority. It is perhaps unsurprising that the general public has largely lost faith in the process.

We should also recognise that this technical process may actually hide or at least disguise the real policy and political choices that are involved in planning decisions, and that government targets over determination timescales and the proportions of schemes delegated to officers have only served to shift the focus even further away from the real purpose of the planning system. However, it is also important that planning decisions taken by members are also justified with reference to published planning policies. This reaffirms the point that planning decisions must be based on a full technical and policy appraisal, but also that there must be accountability for decisions. Any new system introduced must incorporate these two components if transparency and accountability is to be retained or even improved.

One option for ensuring that new structures are transparent and accountable, and that introducing a more 'localist' approach strengthens rather than weakens the planning process and the credibility of both the system and its practitioners, is to make both options and impact appraisals more explicit within both plans and planning application reports. A report summary for a specific planning application should, of course, include a statement of which policy requirements a scheme does not meet (if any) and, if so, why such non-compliance is justified.

However, both plans and planning application reports should include explicit statements of: first, what the alternative development options were and why the proposed option is preferred; and, second, what the impacts of a policy or development proposal are, in terms of negative and positive impacts, including analysis of differential impacts, that is, who (individuals or interest groups) benefits from a scheme and who (individuals or interest groups) receives disbenefits. This appraisal must go beyond the neighbourhood and the more immediate policy or scheme effects. This will make explicit the choices made by the planning bodies both proposing plans and granting planning consent. Any devolution of planning powers either within the existing governance structures or under any new 'localist community-based' structures must incorporate these components.

Key policy options

The key policy directions that must be pursued by national government, whether under the current or a new administration, are as follows.

Focus on providing more affordable homes

The government should not further inflate effective demand for market homes. Such an approach wastes public sector resources and inflates housing prices, making housing even more unaffordable to the majority of households. Subsiding one select group to become homeowners just disadvantages other prospective homeowners, both now and in the future. The critical challenge for any future government is to significantly increase housing supply, with the focus needing to be on both reducing the price of homes in the market available to first-time buyers and, even more critically, increasing the supply of new homes for those who do not have the resources to access the housing market. This means that the majority of new homes, especially in higher-cost areas, should be homes for rent that are affordable by lower-income households and not homes either for market sales or market rent, or that are only marginally sub-market rent or sale. The first action for any incoming government should be to switch subsidies for sub-market homeownership, shared ownership and so-called 'affordable rent' at up to 80% of market rent to social rented homes (ie homes at 'target' rent levels or lower). The long-term objective should be to move from the current position of increasing expenditure on providing welfare benefits to households so that they can access unaffordable housing to using investment subsidies to make housing affordable by lower-income households without dependence on welfare support. This is a much more effective use of government resources and focuses on funding investment in public sector assets rather than funding short-term consumption by individual households. However, it is important to recognise that this is not a short-term transition and housing benefits have to be maintained to support market rents until such a time as a significant additional supply of genuinely affordable housing is available to and accessible by lower-income households. Proposals for an instant transfer from revenue subsidy to capital subsidy or for each local authority to have flexibility to choose between the balance of capital and revenue support are both unworkable as: first, we need several years of new supply of lower-rented homes before households will be able to move from benefit-supported higher-rented accommodation; and, second, the availability of lower-rented homes or benefit support to access higher-rented homes should operate on a nationally consistent basis and should not be dependent on local political discretion as this would have dramatic localised differential 'postcode' lottery impacts, and dramatic impacts on both households' housing options and on the labour market. A transition from 'benefits to 'bricks' will be a 30-year process, and will mean high transitional costs as funding will be required for both bricks and benefits during the transitional period.

The appropriate definition of affordable housing is housing where costs (rent and service charges) do not exceed 30% of the net household income of the lowest-quartile households (this was the definition included in the original 2004 London Plan). This baseline may need adjustment in relation to household size and dwelling size, but rent setting should not be fixed on a household-specific basis. The objective should be to fix a rent at a level that the majority of lower-income households can afford without reliance on benefit, thus reducing reliance on benefit for the lowest-income households – perhaps the lowest decile.

It is best if the term 'affordable housing', which has been so abused in recent years, is abandoned, and the separate concepts of 'social housing' (housing affordable by lower-income households at low rents with secure tenancies) and 'intermediate housing' (housing that is either sub-market rented or shared ownership, or discounted market housing for households unable to access open market housing) are reintroduced. Local planning authorities could then, through their planning policies, set appropriate housing cost ranges and income ranges for different products.

The loss of the existing social housing supply must be stopped. The continuation of the Right to Buy provisions acts as a disincentive to local authorities who are either directly or indirectly supporting the provision of new social housing. Reforms to Right to Buy such as changing eligibility rules or modifying discount arrangements are insufficient. There can be no justification for subsidising individual capital gain from the subsidised disposal of public assets, which reduces the availability of council homes for future households in need and leads to significant expenditure for the public purse in terms of the cost of providing temporary accommodation or housing benefit to house such households in the private sector. No reforms will ensure the funding of equivalent replacement homes from the sales receipts. Therefore, the Right to Buy should be abolished in England, as has already been achieved in Scotland and is being proposed by the Welsh Assembly. A number of reports have put forward proposals for modifying eligibility or discounts, most notably, Murie (2016). While these options may be seeking to achieve political acceptability, in the current crisis of the shortage of affordable housing, there is no justification either for the loss of such housing or for any subsidy from the public sector to individual purchasers. If there was no overall shortage, disposal based on a 1:1 replacement may have some justification, at least in terms of minimising negative impacts, but that is not the current situation in most of the country.

A new approach to strategic planning

There needs to be an effective spatial planning system at the national, regional and local level that incorporates a comprehensive assessment of housing required for all household types and in all sectors, and where targets for new housing supply are based on a consistent approach to identify capacity for residential development that meets the criteria for sustainable residential quality.

Implementation of the Community Infrastructure Levy (CIL) should be dependent on it being demonstrated that its introduction will neither delay appropriate development nor reduce the quantity and quality of affordable housing output. As an alternative to levying CIL or planning contributions at commencement, local authorities should consider the possibility of taking an equity stake in any future value appreciation. While this can be achieved through land disposal covenants or through the establishment of joint venture vehicles, the government should amend planning powers to allow local authorities to take an equity stake in a private development as a condition of planning consent. This would be a constructive alternative to both the current system of planning obligations through section 106 agreements and the proposed CIL, and could replace both regimes. This would ensure that a development is not delayed by onerous initial obligations. It will protect the public sector interest in terms of benefiting from any long-term value appreciation.

The current position of the market is leading to a restructuring of the private house-building sector. This presents new opportunities for land assembly and the procurement of development contracts. The parcelling up of land for development by a range of developers, rather than reliance on a single developer, can both spread development risk and ensure a range of types and styles of housing provision. It could also reduce the negative impact of local landownership monopolies. The UK could benefit from the experience of some other European countries.

The government should establish minimum qualitative and space standards applicable to all new residential development, with exceptions only permitted in clearly specified exceptional circumstances. New development and refurbishment should be to the highest energy standards consistent with value-for-money principles, using available demonstrable experience from other countries (particularly European) to inform how best to reduce carbon emissions, energy bills and fuel poverty. New skills are needed by planners and by those in related professions. Planners need to be fully aware of all the factors that impact on the delivery of housing and the deliverability of planning applications. This includes knowledge of housing market factors, funding arrangements and development viability. Government and academic institutions should focus on supporting relevant higher education courses and Continuous Professional Development (CPD) provision. The government must ensure that planning policy and guidance is realistic. The plan-making system needs to be speedier, with the ability for plans to be reviewed quickly in response to changing external factors. The government should promote the positive role of planning and the importance of collaboration with other professions. There is also a need to recognise the importance of both development management and effective plan-making and monitoring, as well as developing appropriate mechanisms for plan implementation.

Using existing public bodies more effectively

In considering the option of establishing new organisations, it is important to understand the functions and powers of existing public bodies. In this context, it should be noted that the Homes and Communities Agency (HCA) already has extensive powers to fund (through both capital grants and repayable loans) both housing (the provision of new homes, the improvement of existing homes and estate regeneration) and infrastructure. It has the power to fund housing associations, cooperatives, local authorities, arm's-length management organisations (ALMOs) and private developers who register with it and who meet funding criteria. The mayor of London has parallel powers in relation to development in London. The HCA also has compulsory purchase powers (which are rarely, if ever, used), and under the Housing and Regeneration Act 2008, the secretary of state can designate the HCA as the authority for a specified area – a power that has never been used. It was introduced as a reserve power for government to use should a local planning authority seek to obstruct a major strategic government initiative, and was introduced to support the eco-towns programme before the new government decided that this and similar initiatives should not be imposed on local authorities.

The mayor of London has compulsory purchase powers, which are not limited to Mayoral Development Corporation (MDC) areas (London Legacy DC and Old Oak Common DC, currently being established), but can be applied more widely and may be used in the case of mayoral housing zones, which are currently under consideration – proposals having been invited but no designations made as yet. The government has recently decided to establish its own DC for Ebbsfleet, with the secretary of state appointing the DC board. The Ebbsfleet model, having no plan-making functions and with limited capacity for landownership and land value capture, is much more limited than the garden city or new town models and is not necessarily an appropriate model for planning and managing the development of major new settlements.

One option currently being pursued under city deal discussions is the possible transfer of HCA powers and resources to city-regional groupings of authorities (using combined authority arrangements) or to individual urban local authorities. Local authorities operating under combined authority arrangements can choose to exercise plan-making powers on a collaborative basis. Local authorities already have a range of Compulsory Purchase Order powers, so there is no need to transfer this power from the HCA. It is therefore questionable as to what additional powers either the HCA or individual local authorities require, and there is the issue that the HCA and local authorities could make more effective use of their existing powers. Current constraints relate mainly to: the issue of the financing of development in terms of the insufficiency of government grants; limitations on the ability to raise finance through taxation (the restrictions on council tax increases, while the HCA has no tax-raising powers); the limitations on local authority borrowing (the HCA has no independent borrowing capacity); and the financial rules relating to the compulsory acquisition of land that require purchase at the market value for the proposed end use, rather than the pre-existing use value. Some of these matters are considered in the following.

The key point is that without changes on these fundamental constraints, there is limited benefit from setting up new organisations such as MDCs. On the other hand, there are major disbenefits, including a considerable set-up cost, a hiatus in which key development decisions cannot be made until the new body is fully operational and, in some cases, difficult relationships with agencies from whom powers have been transferred, together with concerns about democratic accountability. This is often followed within a few years by the winding down of the new agency, generally with the development incomplete or, in some cases (eg in the case of the Thurrock DC), hardly started.

In the past, there have been three main reasons for setting up new organisations: first, where central government has been of the view that the local government bodies are either opposed to the development proposal or that they lack the competence or capacity to take the project forward (the key justification for setting up the London Docklands DC); second, where the project involves development in a number of local authority areas and requires a consistent approach to delivery within a fixed timescale that is not constrained by the different policies or procedural arrangements of the existing local authorities (the key justification for the establishment of the Olympic Delivery Agency, though it should be recognised that much of the preparatory work was undertaken on a collaborative basis by the four main London boroughs concerned); and, third, where the project cannot be funded from the local authority's resources or from available central government subsidies, and requires private finance beyond the borrowing capacity of the local authority (which is itself limited by central government controls) – this would normally require some form of private-sector-led body, though this may be a joint venture company in which the local authority has a minority interest. In the latter case, the initiative to set up a new body may be an initiative by the local authority rather than by central government.

The HCA currently combines funding and regulatory functions, which is necessary to ensure the effective use of public resources. Regulation needs to be enhanced to protect tenants' interests as well as public investment. There remains an anomaly that in London, the mayor is funder while the HCA retains the regulatory function. This points to the difficulty of a rolling programme of transferring functions to other agencies across England. The government still needs to determine the distribution of resources between different parts of the country and it is important that in order to ensure the effective use of resources, there is some link between resource allocation and the use of resources. The government and specifically the HCA have increasingly moved away from a resource allocation system that reflects either the spatial distribution of unmet housing requirements or the spatial distribution of the assessed development capacity, to a bid-based regime where the government through the HCA allocates resources in response to bids, primarily on the basis of which provider can provide the most homes for the least government subsidy.

The city deals approach to resource allocation and the devolution of powers now being operated by central government in relation to individual local authorities or groups of local authorities has the same risk of distributing resources not to the areas of greatest need, but instead to the areas of most effective lobbying and where political returns can be maximised. This is disguised under the banner of 'localism' but loses both transparency and any consistency of resource and policy response to the needs arising in different parts of the country. It does not lead to the most effective use of resources and is unfair in terms of both the differential treatment of local authorities and, more critically, the varying ability of different authorities to respond adequately to meeting the statutory responsibilities within their functional and geographical areas of responsibility.

Some new initiatives, such as the previous mayor of London's housing zones, do not involve new statutory powers for new organisations, but relate to the concentrated use of existing powers (including powers not previously used) in specific geographical areas. They may or may not lead to a change in the spatial distribution of funding resources. However, zoning initiatives of this kind should not be confused with the establishment of new organisational structures. Similarly the Coalition government's garden cities initiative, inviting proposals for new garden cities, was primarily a publicity or branding exercise as the initiative involved neither new powers nor new resources to support any such proposals. Not surprisingly, the initiative, like many similar initiatives in the past, has attracted little interest and has not been progressed.

The key questions therefore are: what are the benefits and disbenefits of transferring powers and/or resources from one agency or another? What can a new organisation do that the current organisation cannot? Can the delivery objective be more effectively delivered by either more effectively resourcing an existing agency to utilise its existing powers or, where an agency is not utilising its powers effectively, using statutory powers to require it to do so? Any new government needs to have these questions in mind before initiating any organisational changes, including further devolutionary measures.

There may therefore be a case for establishing new housing and infrastructure organisations where existing organisations cannot deliver, even with enhanced powers and funding. Any such organisations should be established on a longer-term basis (eg for 30 years), should be established in collaboration with existing local statutory bodies within the area, should operate within a structure of clear democratic accountability and should have the powers to raise private finance as well as to receive grants and loans from central government and other public sector bodies.

Strategic planning and the right to grow

The current planning framework does not ensure adequate planning on an inter-authority basis and has demonstrated significant failure, especially in being unable to ensure a planned response to the needs of growing populations in constrained and underbounded local authority areas. The duty to cooperate provisions of the Localism Act 2011 have been insufficient to ensure the delivery of the required collaborative planning between neighbouring authorities. This has become critical given the abolition (beyond London) of any statutory framework for regional and sub-regional planning, with arrangements in the London metropolitan region also being unsatisfactory given that the mayor of London's planning powers are limited to part of the metropolitan functional urban region or travel-to-work area.

It is necessary to set out the mechanisms for delivering the concept of the 'right to grow'. There is logic in extending the administrative boundaries of growing urban areas to include both the existing developed periphery and sufficient area to provide for projected population growth for, say, the next 50 years. However, the process for boundary changes can be lengthy, and in the shorter term, a new collaborative approach between underbounded authorities and their neighbouring local planning authorities is essential.

While local authorities have the power to plan on a collaborative basis, they are not required to do so. While local enterprise partnerships provide a framework for collaboration between public and private sector organisations, their focus is primarily on inward investment and economic growth and not on the wider range of planning objectives. They are not statutory bodies and have no planning functions. More important still, they have no direct electoral basis and thus lack legitimacy in the eyes of citizens. Local authorities can already work collaboratively on strategic planning matters under the provisions of the Planning and Compulsory Purchase Act 2004 to produce and adopt joint plans, and some are now jointly implementing strategic planning functions under combined authority powers. However, there is no requirement on authorities to collaborate, with the consequence that under what is effectively a voluntary system, some local planning authorities are able to opt out of any effective collaborative planning arrangements. This is most problematic where a constrained authority seeks assistance from a less constrained neighbouring authority only to find its approaches rejected. In practice, this has led to a number of local plans being rejected by inspectors at public inquiry because there has been little evidence of effective collaboration, which has, on occasions, not been the fault of the presenting authority.

A plan can be rejected because it does not meet local needs within its authority area, but can also be rejected because it has failed to take into account the needs of a neighbouring authority. However, the government has not specified which authorities need to collaborate or specified the appropriate geographical areas for such cooperation, whether based on travel-to-work areas or other criteria. Decisions of both planning inspectors and the secretary of state have not been consistent on this matter because while there is guidance on the process of meeting the duty to cooperate provisions of the Localism Act, there is no guidance on how policy conflicts can be resolved, notably, in relation to the key issues of differential housing requirements, development capacity and potential mismatches within a travel-to-work area.

These conflicts become more problematic as there is now no structure for regional planning and housing and employment growth targets in England. The regional planning framework established in 2004 was not given sufficient time to demonstrate its potential value, with its abolition following the election of the Coalition government in 2010, an abolition process that took three years to fully implement, with the regional planning organisations actually being disbanded well before the regional plans were formally withdrawn, causing considerable confusion as to whether or not the plan targets remained in effect. There is now (excepting London) no regional assessment of either need or capacity and no statutory planning framework for setting sub-regional priorities or for assessing the contribution of local authority-level policies and targets to meeting wider needs. There is no statutory framework for planning housing, employment, transport or infrastructure provision across a region or sub-region. The Coalition government was hostile to regional governance structures and any concept of regionalism. Department of Communities and Local Government data are generally no longer published on a regional basis and the terms 'more than local' or 'sub-national' are now used rather than the terms 'sub-regional' or 'regional'.

England is also the only major country in Western Europe that has no national spatial plan. Scotland, Wales and Northern Ireland all have national spatial plans and some structure for regional or city-regional planning. The current government's localist perspective means that there is neither a government regional policy or any national perspective on the spatial distribution of residential or employment growth. In this context, national government policy decisions on major infrastructure investment, such as High Speed 2, work within a policy vacuum in which there is no assessment of the extent to which infrastructure investment supports employment or residential growth in specific locations. From the perspective of ensuring the most cost-effective use of public resources, such an approach appears grossly irresponsible. It must surely be the responsibility of a national government to set out spatially related priorities for the use of central government resources, including resources raised from taxation, in terms of an assessment of potential long-term social, economic and environmental impact.

It is inappropriate and bluntly irresponsible for any planning minister to express the view that the location of employment, housing or infrastructure should be primarily dependent on whether the existing residents of an area welcome the proposition. In fact, the government is now largely reliant on local councils and local communities themselves to put forward proposals for growth. There is therefore now no national assessment of the spatial distribution of the employment, housing or infrastructure requirements arising from population growth and migration, and consequently no ability to plan funding to support this assessment. Instead, the government seeks to react to the uncontrolled growth that may take place. The consequence is that in some locations, there is a surplus of resources and capacity, and in other areas, there is a deficit. The government's view is that the market will self-correct. In practice, this means that the government will shift resources to the areas that are economically strong and growing, but provide no support to the areas in decline, and funding is often in arrears rather than assisting local authorities to undertake upfront investment in social infrastructure such as education and health facilities.

The government's regional economic planning and regeneration strategy, so far as it has one, is to support the winners while not seeking to mitigate disadvantage in the declining areas, so it is not surprising that the economic differentials between the South East and most of the rest of the UK are increasing rather than reducing. This trend is being reinforced by the very uneven cuts in local government spending and the retreat from equalisation in the local government finance system. The previous objective of seeking to reduce regional inequity has long since been abandoned. As set out in the Lyons report, a key priority for a new government should be to initiate a process for producing a national spatial plan and for indicating areas of the country with a potential for employment and residential growth (not necessarily limited to the greater South East) as a basis for national infrastructure planning, while, at the same time, identifying measures to support communities in decline and interventions that could at least stabilise the position, if not reverse the decline, so that communities in these areas are not further disadvantaged.

Within this new context of national spatial planning, which needs to include a regional dimension and a regional-level analysis and monitoring system (though not necessarily a reconstitution of the pre-existing regional planning bodies), there is a simple mechanism for establishing a democratically accountable basis for planning at the sub-regional/city-regional level. The government should determine groupings of local planning authorities based on travel-to-work areas. This should use a statistically sound methodology that is not dependent on individual local authority choice of partners. A methodology was proposed in a report by Jones, Coombes and Wong, commissioned by the National Housing and Planning Advisory Unit and published by the Department of Communities and Local Government (DCLG) in 2010 (DCLG, 2010b). The government should bring in legislation to impose a statutory duty on the groups of authorities to use their combined authority powers to draft and adopt a strategic sub-regional plan. The grouping would include district and unitary planning authorities and any county council within the area that retained powers in relation to the planning of transport, minerals and waste.

The sub-regional strategic plan should be based on a combined authority sub-regional assessment of development requirements (housing, employment and infrastructure) and a combined assessment of development capacity for all development requirements consistent with economic, social and environmental sustainable development criteria. These studies need to be on a consistent basis in line with a methodology to be published by the central government, which ensures consistent criteria and assessment both within sub-regions and between sub-regions. These strategic plans would need to operate within the framework of the national spatial plan and include targets and site allocations to fully meet the identified employment, housing and infrastructure provision targets within the sub-regional area. Where such requirements are not fully met, the planning inspector and the secretary of state would have the power to amend the plan. This framework could be established by relatively minor changes to the current planning legislation, would not require any new organisations to be established and would operate within the current structure of democratic accountability.

It is also necessary to touch on the relationship between the need for strategic planning and the current focus on localism, demonstrated most explicitly through the neighbourhood planning provisions within the Localism Act 2011. While it is appropriate for existing residents to be involved in the process of planning an area, it is important to recognise that: first, the planning of a new urban area cannot be based solely on the interests or aspirations of the existing residential community (or a group of individuals within that community); and, second, that it should not be possible for any group of residents to obstruct the delivery of a local authority plan already adopted and based on an evidence base, extensive consultation, public inquiry, independent assessment by an inspector and a democratic decision at the local authority level, and demonstrating conformity with national planning policy, so far as that exists. At present, there is considerable confusion as to the relationship between neighbourhood plans and local plans, which has seriously limited the effectiveness of both the neighbourhood planning and local planning processes.

For the neighbourhood planning system to be retained and to make a constructive contribution to both plan-making and implementation, a government needs to issue much clearer guidance on what planning matters can be determined in a neighbourhood plan, and the strategic policies within a local plan with which a neighbourhood plan should conform. While it may be appropriate for a neighbourhood group to express a view on what is an appropriate development on a specific site, it is not appropriate for a group to seek to obstruct the delivery of strategic objectives. This requires the local authority plan to be explicit about development objectives and targets for specific neighbourhoods, which would allow the neighbourhood plan to propose alternative sites for delivering the targets set. This would enable neighbourhood groups to have a significant impact on the location and form of development without jeopardising the ability of the local authority to implement its local plan and to deliver development in order to meet its assessment of development requirements.

To extend the existing neighbourhood planning system without clarifying the relationship between neighbourhood and local plans both limits the ability of local authorities to implement their plans and carry out their statutory responsibilities, and weakens the democratic basis of the planning framework, while also allowing for the possibility that neighbourhood interests will block development from which more disadvantaged households might benefit. Unless there are constraints on neighbourhood planning, there is a risk that the system will be used primarily to protect neighbourhood interests, which brings with it the risk of increased social polarisation.

Land acquisition and compulsory purchase

As recognised in the Lyons report (Labour Party, 2014), one of the key factors in the high price of housing is land cost. Much, if not most, of the land suitable for housing development is in private sector ownership. In some cases, local authorities own little developable land, and sites suitable for development may be in multiple ownership. In some cases, local authorities need to take a more proactive role in land assembly. The main constraint in local authority land purchase is the requirement, whether under compulsory purchase or other legislation, that the local authority must pay for land on the basis of the intended use. Consequently, for a local authority to acquire agricultural land on the edge of a developed area may mean that the local authority has to pay housing value of £3 million per hectare rather than agricultural value of £30,000 per hectare. In central London, acquisition costs can be £100 million per hectare or more. The government recognises that existing CPO procedures can obstruct the development of major infrastructure projects, and the Chancellor of the Exchequer has recently proposed that compensation should be on the basis of an amount higher than market value. In relation to housing, however, a landowner can receive an uplift in value of 10,000% or more arising from the zoning of land in agricultural use for housing.

As suggested by the Lyons report (Labour Party, 2014), there needs to be a cap on the value uplift accruing to the landowner. As the value increment arises solely from investment by others (public and private) and from a planning decision made by the local authority, it is appropriate that the benefit of the increase in value accrues to the community as a whole rather than solely to the landowner. In theory, the price paid by a developer for land should be constrained by the planning policy applying to the development site. For example, if there is a requirement for a site to provide 50% of new development as affordable housing, then this should constrain the price paid for the land. Similarly, the price should be discounted to reflect obligations to provide infrastructure to support the development. However, in practice, the land price paid may not reflect this policy context, particularly where the policy context for such obligations is weakened. The Lyons report suggested that a CPO should be based on the land value plus a generous premium. One option is for the premium to be set at a fixed percentage over pre-existing use value – say 20%. A more sensitive approach would be to set differential percentage uplifts relating to the pre-existing land use and/or the value of the pre-existing land use, so the premium for the landowner for low-value land would be, in percentage terms, higher than the premium for higher-value land, for example, a 100% uplift could be allowed on land with a pre-existing use value of £30,000 a hectare, but only a 10% uplift on land with a value of £1 million a hectare, and 5% for land with a value of £10 million a hectare. A third alternative would be that the landowner is initially paid only the pre-existing use value for land but offered an equity stake in the value of the development on completion.

It is preferable for development land to be brought into public ownership at some stage during the development process so that the landowners do not realise the full value uplift arising from planning zoning or planning consent. It is therefore proposed that where a landowner refuses to sell a development site in line with the terms set out earlier within a defined timescale, the local authority should be able to acquire the land at existing use value. This will act as an incentive to the landowner to implement the planned development or to accept the local authority's offer, which is on a more generous basis. The CPO power should apply to any land that has been zoned for residential development. The local authority could therefore either develop the land directly or sell on the land to an appropriate developer under a covenant setting out conditions on development output, as considered later.

It should also be recognised that public sector organisations also own land suitable for housing development. This is not limited to local planning authorities, but includes the mayor of London, the HCA, health trusts and government departments such as the Ministry of Defence. In recent years, these agencies have generally sought to dispose of sites to the private sector for maximum receipts. In some cases, local authorities have relaxed planning policy requirements in relation to affordable housing in order to maximise the receipt. This is not good practice and creates a precedent for privately led schemes.

There is a case for requiring local authorities and other agencies to first consider the potential for 'surplus' land to meet public policy objectives before the land is released to the market. It may be appropriate for the local authority or other public body to develop land directly, or if selling the land, only sell on a leasehold basis or retain an equity stake in the completed development so that part of any increase in value is repayable to the local authority. Where land is sold to a developer, the land disposal covenant should put strict requirements on the form of development, including, where appropriate, restrictions on sale prices and/or rent levels, which would ensure that the housing developed is affordable over the longer term, as well as initial sales and rentals, to lower- and middle-income households.

Development viability

The current focus on development viability is limiting the ability of local authorities to use the planning system to achieve planning policy objectives, especially in relation to the provision of affordable homes and social infrastructure to support new residential development. The focus in the *National planning policy framework* (NPPF) (DCLG, 2012) on the right of landowners and developers to receive competitive returns on their investment is problematic as 'competitive' is not defined. The NPPF also states that the local authority should not, through planning policy, planning obligations or CIL, impose costs on a developer that lead to a scheme being non-viable. The government also introduced a procedure by which a developer who had already received planning consent for a development and had agreed a level of planning obligations could seek for this agreement to be amended or waived on the basis that the scheme was now less viable than at the time consent was granted. This inhibits the enabling role of the local planning authority when there are changes to the market or the financial system, such as a decrease in land values or a reduction in house prices.

The proposals set out earlier on land assembly and CPOs cover the issue of landowners' return and the basis on which land costs should be eligible for inclusion in a development viability assessment. This would avoid developers including significant 'hope value' in their land purchase price and consequently in their financial appraisal submission. However, it is also necessary for the government to set a norm rate of return on developer investment, as well as norms for other factors, such as financing costs. One option would be to set an initial allowable return (mark-up) on investment at a fixed proportion, for example, 15%. This allowance and other cost assumptions could be reviewed by central government on an annual basis. This would allow for a consistent basis of development appraisal between developers and local authorities, and would act as a basis for the consideration of appeals by planning inspectors or by the secretary of state.

Land acquisition costs in viability assessments should have regard to planning policy. It should not be acceptable for a developer to claim land costs based on an assumption that planning policies would not apply in full. It is therefore important that local authorities actually apply their adopted planning policies to individual development applications, rather than create precedents that encourage a landowner and/or developer to assume higher values. Local authorities should therefore not allow developers to build developments that are over-developments relative to published planning policy on site context and density, nor should developers be allowed to progress schemes on the basis of a different mix from that specified in a site planning brief or that do not meet the local authority's affordable housing targets. Where a planning application is refused on the grounds of failing to comply with published policy and the developer does not put forward a policy-compliant proposal within six months, the local authority should have the right to acquire the site compulsorily on the basis of the value assumptions set out earlier.

The provisions of the Housing and Regeneration Act 2008 for a developer to seek the revision of a planning agreement that they have signed should be repealed. Local authorities should be allowed to impose a planning condition on a development requiring a proportion of any value uplift arising above the values assumed in the financial appraisal to be paid to the local authority.

All viability appraisals should be transparent, with full information available to planning officers, councillors and public scrutiny. This is in line with recent judgements of the information commissioner and the courts. There remains justifiable public concern as to the abuse of the viability appraisal system by developers, and that local planning authorities have been increasingly disempowered in the negotiation process. There is a case for a government review of the viability appraisal system and its role in planning, with the government to publish guidance on the application of viability assessments and the assumptions to be used within them. One possible option is for the application of affordable housing targets to specific developments not being subject to a viability appraisal, and that policy targets are rigorously required on all development sites to which they apply. This would then require developers to take into account the full policy requirements applying before determining the payment that they are prepared to make for the land. Where a developer is not willing to proceed with development on this basis, the local planning authority should compulsorily acquire the site and fund the costs of affordable housing directly.

Financing new development

One option is to increase the ability of local authorities to incur borrowing against their own assets or income streams under prudential borrowing arrangements. Local authorities or groups of local authorities should be able to establish investment funds, raising finance from a range of private sources, including individual investors, to finance both housing development and infrastructure provision.

The government could convert the Public Sector Works Loan Board into a housing and infrastructure financing bank in order to provide finance, secured against national assets, at a rate lower than market rates. Another option is for local authorities and groupings of local authorities to establish municipal investment corporations to bring together public and private investment resources to fund major housing schemes and local infrastructure delivery. These would be exempt from centrally imposed borrowing limits, subject to demonstrating compliance with the principles of prudential borrowing.

The provision of new good-quality homes and the renovation of the existing social housing stock for lower-income households cannot be financed entirely through borrowing from other public or private sources as costs are not repayable solely from rent income (whether or not part of this is itself supported by housing benefit). It is therefore necessary for the government to recognise that, in some circumstances, investment in the form of grants rather than repayable loans is appropriate. This is investment in that such grants create housing, which is an asset that, subject to maintenance, will appreciate over time.

We should seek to avoid financing mechanisms that rely on the disposal of public assets. Housing investment reduces revenue costs to the public sector, not just in terms of savings in housing benefit, but in terms of savings in health, education and criminal justice costs. Any appraisal of the costs and benefits of different levels and forms of housing investment should have regard to these factors.

A municipal investment corporation would provide the confidence to private investors that funds will go into projects that have a good chance of achieving their stated objectives, and also incentivise local authorities to promote and support strategic developments that might otherwise be unpopular with their electorate (Falk, 2014). These could be modelled on the Dutch Bank Nederlendse Gemeenten (BNG), which was set up by local authorities and the government together; the corporation could act as an adjunct of a British investment bank. It would develop the role of the Municipal Bonds Agency that the Local Government Association set up in 2014 (LGA, 2014).

Such an agency, along with the power to assemble land at close to existing use value, will be crucial to achieving the doubling of house-building that Labour is committed to. However, just as importantly, it will help to fund the upgrades in local infrastructure (energy, waste, water and transport) that are essential to areas growing in a sustainable way. In all considerations of funding streams and attracting additional 'investment' into housing, an overriding concern should be to ensure that the additional funds lead directly and only to additional physical output (including refurbishment), avoiding adding to demand pressures on the housing stock, which inflate housing and land prices.

A tax and regulatory regime that supports the effective use of housing supply

The current land and property tax regime is not conducive to supporting the development of new homes and to ensuring the effective use of new homes. A significant proportion of the existing housing stock is not used effectively. This imbalance in the distribution of the housing stock is growing as under-occupation increases at the same time as overcrowding. We do not endorse the view that rationalising the existing use of the country's housing stock will itself solve the housing shortage, as argued by Danny Dorling (2014). Nevertheless, the issue of excessive under-occupation does need to be tackled.

The same could be said for tenure conditions. Homes that are currently unavailable to many households in housing need due to upfront costs, rent levels or not being fit for purpose as a family home because they are let on a short-term tenancy or with prejudicial lettings policies could make a more effective contribution to housing supply through stronger regulation, thus reducing the requirement to build more homes. The better regulation of lettings agents or tenure and rent reform in the private rented sector could also make a positive contribution.

The current development tax regime, comprising the optional CIL and local negotiated planning obligations, acts as a tax on development gains, while undeveloped land is not subject to taxation. Taxation should incentivise development. Consequently, there is a case for introducing a tax on land that is appropriate for development, including both allocated and consented land, in order to encourage the landowner to bring the land forward for development.

While there remains a case for taxing private sector value appreciation that arises as a result of land allocation, planning or adjacent development and infrastructure, the current mechanisms for taxing value appreciation at the time of starting on site can act as a deterrent to development. There is logic in only taxing value appreciation from a new development at the point at which the value appreciation has actually been realised, that is, at completion and/or onward disposal. There is therefore an argument that deferring the payment of CIL and planning obligations to completion or disposal will assist in the delivery of new development. Value growth, furthermore, tends to continue through the life of any scheme, especially large schemes, and a satisfactory value-capture regime should aim to generate a public sharing in this continuing growth.

An alternative approach is for the local planning authority to take an equity share in a private development as a condition of planning consent, so that a proportion of any value lift, either during the construction period or at initial disposal or subsequent further disposal, is payable to the local planning authority. This will allow the local planning authority to establish a recyclable investment fund to support new infrastructure and housing development.

Property taxes also urgently need reform. The main property taxes comprise stamp duty, formally known as 'stamp duty land transaction tax', and council tax. Stamp duty is a tax on purchase, which is a tax on a household at the time when they are most extended financially. There is a case to be considered for replacing stamp duty with a tax on capital gain on disposal. Capital gains tax would be levied at the point at which capital gains are realised. It currently applies to second homes and to properties where the landlord is non-resident. Application of capital gains tax to first homes would reduce the ability of a homeowner to use their capital gain to trade up and buy a larger property, generally in excess of any normal space requirement. However, this would have a negative impact on a household seeking to plan ahead for a growing family. It would also reduce the ability of households to pass on property wealth to their relatives. The transfer of property wealth between generations is now one of the most significant drivers of growing inequity in wealth and access to services, and the limiting of such transfers, and parallel changes, to inheritance tax thresholds would make a significant contribution to reversing this trend, as well as leading to a slowdown in house price inflation and in house price to income ratios that have excluded many middle-income households from housing markets. However, tax thresholds would need to be set at a level that focused taxation on households with higher levels of assets rather than penalising households on the margins of homeownership. Specific proposals would need a sophisticated modelling of both impact and revenue generated before implementation.

Council tax is a tax on the occupation of dwellings, and in England (in contrast with Wales), is based on values as at 1991. Council tax rates do not therefore reflect the significant increase in residential property values since that date. The highest council tax band, band H, applies to properties with a value of £320,000 as at 1991. This compares with an average current property value in London of over £500,000 (in Wales, a revaluation was carried out in 2005). It is essential that a revaluation of residential property for council tax purposes is undertaken. Modern data systems and modelling techniques would now enable valuations to be recalculated annually and automatically, thus both economising on valuation costs and keeping the tax base up to date, just as we do for other taxes. It is also essential that higher-value tax bands are created. This will ensure that tax reflects the value of property and will also significantly increase the resources available to local authorities, thus reducing their dependence on central government grant. It is also suggested that to ensure the most effective use of both new and existing housing stock, the tax should include a factor relating to the level of occupation of a property. This would act as an incentive to under-occupiers to either take in lodgers or move to smaller accommodation. However, as in the case of other potential tax options, there would be a need for the modelling of options to assess potential negative impacts.

It is recognised that no single tax can incentivise the bringing forward of land for appropriate development, ensure public benefit from land value appreciation arising from planning decisions and ensure the effective use of the new and existing housing stock. A land tax will not on its own achieve all these objectives.

Summary of the required reform programme

Immediate legislation

- Repeal the Housing and Planning Act 2016 (except for the rogue landlord clauses).

Investment

- Stop all forms of subsidy, whether direct or indirect (including any subsidy on land disposal), to owner-occupied properties and new development for individual or corporate private ownership.

- Any financial assistance by the government for homeownership or private rented housing should be in the form of an equity stake by a public body, with the equity stake repayable to that public body, that is, the public body receives its share in any value uplift on resale.
- Discounted sale of council and housing association homes constitutes a subsidy to homeownership, by which the purchaser makes the capital gain, and should be terminated.
- The starter homes initiative, which also involves financial support for home purchasers, who can then capitalise on the market value at sale, representing a 20% uplift on the purchase price plus any other gain in market value, should also be terminated.
- The government should reinstate a programme of grants for its social rented provision through councils and housing associations on the basis of secure tenancies and controlled rents. The level of grant should be on the basis of covering the capital costs of development not covered by capitalised rent income over a 60-year period. This, in effect, would be a reintroduction of the mixed funding regime operating on a system of cost indicators, as operated by the former Housing Corporation. Borrowing by the council or housing association would then be entirely fundable from rent income without recourse to the need to cross-subsidise from other sources, such as through agreements with developers, income from the sale of market homes or shared-ownership equity, or the disposal of other assets.
- Government limits on local authority borrowing to support investment should be removed and replaced by a prudential borrowing regime where local authorities and other public sector bodies can borrow against the security of their assets and income.

Planning and land

- The government should draw up a national spatial plan that identifies general locations for residential and employment growth supported by planned transport, social and utilities infrastructure. The national spatial plan would need to ensure consistency between social, economic and environmental sustainability objectives and be an integrated housing, employment, infrastructure, transport and environmental plan. It would guide national decisions on infrastructure funding and set a framework for the development of regional, sub-regional and local plans.

- Local planning authorities should be required to allocate housing sites to meet the full housing requirements in their area or, where this is not possible, reach agreement with neighbouring authorities in their sub-regional or city-regional planning area as to the identification of residential development capacity.

- The government should determine joint planning areas based on travel-to-work areas. A statutory requirement should be imposed on the authorities within each area to undertake a combined assessment of housing requirements and development capacity, and they should agree on site allocations, based on consistent density and sustainable development criteria. Where agreement cannot be reached, central government should have the power to determine local planning authority residential development targets and site allocations.

- Local planning authorities should be required to prepare planning briefs for all housing sites, setting out the requirements for built form, density, dwelling size and type, and tenure/affordability based on the assessment of housing requirements in their area. Development proposals that are not in conformity with these briefs should be refused.

- Local planning authorities should have the power to compulsorily acquire any housing site allocated in an approved plan at existing use value.

- Where a local planning authority grants planning consent for a private development, they should have the power to take an equity stake in the development, as part of any subsequent value uplift is repayable to the authority. This could be used as an alternative to agreeing a planning obligation or requiring the payment of CIL.

- There should be a mandatory new minimum standard for all new residential development, irrespective of tenure or location. This should include internal space standards, amenities standards and environmental standards. These should apply to residential units provided through the conversion of non-residential premises.

Taxation

- Stamp duty on the purchase of residential property should be replaced by a tax on the capital gain on land and property on disposal.
- Inheritance tax should be revised to increase the tax on the transfer of land and residential property through inheritance.
- The option of reintroducing schedule A income tax based on the imputed rental value of owner-occupied dwellings should be considered.
- Valuation of property for the purposes of council tax should be updated to reflect current values. There is also a case for the level of council tax being related more explicitly to the size of the dwelling in terms of floor space.
- Higher rates of tax should be introduced for higher-value property. Rates of tax on individual property should take into account the level of occupation of properties – properties that are under-occupied being subject to a multiplier relating to the level of under-occupation, with penal rates for vacant property.
- There should be no limits on the ability of local authorities to set rates of council tax.

CONCLUSION
THE FOUR KEY ISSUES

Land, ownership, money and power

Land

Development land needs to be under public sector control. Not only should local planning authorities be able to use their planning powers to determine the allowable land use or uses for a specific site, but they should also specify the type of housing to be developed in terms of built form, the size of units, tenure and affordability. Local authorities should have the power to acquire any such site at existing use value and should be able to develop directly or transfer land to another agency for development on conditions it sets.

Ownership

Where a private developer is undertaking development, the local planning authority should take an equity stake in the development so that part of the benefit of value appreciation is paid to the public sector. Such receipts can be used to fund transport and social infrastructure, as well as housing for lower-income households. Public bodies should not dispose of land except where they retain an equity and control the future use of land.

Money

Investment is required to provide housing, even where land costs may be low. Public investment requires subsidy. The ability of public bodies to borrow from the private sector at market rates is not in itself a solution as all borrowing requires repayment. Investment in public assets is an investment in the public good and for future generations.

Power

The balance of power between the public and private sector must be rebalanced. The public sector must manage the use of the private sector as contributors to the delivery of public policy objectives. Both funding decisions and the choice of policy objectives must be through democratically accountable bodies and the basis all decisions must be transparent.

These are fundamental issues, and any proposition, whether from the government, political parties, academics or practitioners, which fails to operate within these parameters will be inadequate.

REFERENCES

Alakeson, V. (2011) *Making a rented house a home*, London: Resolution Foundation.

Alakeson, V., Blacklock, K., Halilovic, C., Rothery, T. and Salisbury, N. (2013) *Building homes for generation rent*, London: Resolution Foundation.

Architects Journal (2014) Britain's shoebox houses. Available at: https://www.architectsjournal.co.uk/news/britains-shoe-box-houses-among-smallest-in-europe/8664402.fullarticle

Atkinson, A. (2015) *Inequality*, Cambridge, MA: Harvard University Press.

Ball, M. (2012) 'Housing supply and planning controls', National Planning and Housing Advisory Unit. Available at: http://webarchive.nationalarchives.gov.uk/20120919132719/www.communities.gov.uk/documents/507390/pdf/1436960.pdf

Barker, K. (2004) *Delivering stability: Securing our future housing needs. Final report of review of housing supply*, London: HMSO.

Bentley, G. and Pugalis, L. (2013) 'New directions in economic development: localist policy discourses and the Localism Act', Local Economy.

Berry, M. (2014) 'Neoliberalism and the city: or the failure of market fundamentalism', *Housing, Theory and Society*, 31(1): 1–18.

Blyth, M. (2015) *Austerity: The history of a dangerous idea*, Oxford: Oxford University Press.

Bowie, D. (2008a) *Housing and the credit crunch: Government and property market failure*, London: COMPASS.

Bowie, D. (2008b) 'Space at home', presentation to RIBA seminar. Available at: https://www.architecture.com/Files/RIBAProfessionalServices/ResearchAndDevelopment/Symposium/2008/DuncanBowie.pdf

Bowie, D. (2010a) *Politics, planning and homes in a world city*, London: Routledge.

Bowie, D. (2015) 'The wrong solution to London's housing crisis', comment on IPPR report, 'City villages'. Available at: https://redbrickblog.wordpress.com/2015/03/31/city-villages-the-wrong-solution-to-londons-housing-crisis/

Bowie, D. (2016a) *The radical and socialist tradition in British planning: From puritan colonies to garden cities*, London: Routledge.

Bowie, D. (2016b) 'Strategic planning in the London metropolitan region', *Town and Country Planning*, 85(8): 304–6.

Bowie, D. (2016c) 'Beyond the Compact City', *Planning in London*, 97(April/June): 59–70. Available at: http://www.planninginlondon.com/assets/PIL97%20UPLOADS/pil97%20BOWIE.pdf

Cheshire, P., Nathan, M., and Overman, H. (2014) *Urban economics and urban policy: Challenging convenyional policy wisdom,* London: Edward Elgar.

COMPASS (no date) 'Good society'. Available at: https://www.compassonline.org.uk/ideas/good-society/

Conservative Party (2009) *Control shift: Returning power to local communities*, London: Conservative Party.

Conservative Party (2010a) *Open source planning*, London: Conservative Party.

Corbyn, J. (2016) 'Speech to Labour Party Conference', 28 September.

Cowan, D. and Marsh, A. (2016) *The battle of the bedroom tax*, Bristol: Policy Press.

DCLG (2009) *Building Britain's future*, ministerial statement, 17 July.

DCLG (2010a) *From big government to big society*, press statement, 12 December.

DCLG (2010b) *Geography of Housing Market Areas.* Report for the Naional Housing and Planning Advice Unit by Colin Jones, Mike Coombes and Cecelia Wong.

DCLG (2011) *Laying the foundations: A housing strategy for England*, London: DCLG.

DCLG (2012) *The national planning policy framework*, London: DCLG.

DCLG (2014) *National planning policy guidance*. Available at: http://planningguidance.planningportal.gov.uk/blog/guidance/duty-to-cooperate/what-is-the-duty-to-cooperate-and-what-does-it-require/

DCLG (2015) 'English housing survey 2013–14'. Available at: https://www.gov.uk/government/collections/english-housing-survey

DCLG (2016a) 'Live tables on housing'. Available at: https://www.gov.uk/government/statistical-data-sets/live-tables-on-housing-

DCLG (2016b) 'English housing survey 2014–15'. Available at: https://www.gov.uk/government/statistics/english-housing-survey-2014-to-2015-headline-report

Dorling, D. (2014) *All that is solid*, London: Allen Lane.

Edwards, M. (2015) *The prospects for land, rent and housing in UK cities,* Government Office for Science, Foresight Programme.

Edwards, M. (2016) 'The housing crisis: too difficult or a great opportunity?', *Soundings*, 62(Alternatives to neoliberalism): 23–42. Available at: https://www.lwbooks.co.uk/soundings/62/the-housing-crisis-too-difficult-or-great-opportunity

Evans, A. and Hartwitch, O. (2005) *Unaffordable housing: Fables and myths,* London: Policy Exchange.

Evening Standard (2015) 'Housing crisis overtakes transport as biggest concern for Londoners', report on YOUGOV poll, 15 April.

Fainstein, S. (2010) *The just city*, Ithaca, NY: Cornell University Press.

Falk, N. (2014) *Funding housing and local growth*, London: Smith Institute. Available at: http://www.smith-institute.org.uk/book/funding-housing-and-local-growth-how-a-british-investment-bank-can-help-2/

GOL(Government Office for London) (2008) Circular 1/2008. *Strategic Planning Functions for London*, London: GOL.

GOS (Government Office for Science) (2010) *Land use futures*, Foresight Report, London: Government Office for Science.

Greater London Authority (GLA) (2016) 'London datastore'. Available at: http://data.london.gov.uk/dataset?groups=housing

Gregory, J. (2009) *In the mix: Narrowing the gap between public and private housing*, London: Fabian Society/Webb Memorial Trust.

Halifax (2016) 'First time buyers review', 23 July. Available at: https://static.halifax.co.uk/assets/pdf/mortgages/pdf/20160723-Halifax-FTB-H1-FINAL.pdf

Harvey, D. (1989) *The urban experience*, Baltimore, MD: Johns Hopkins Press.

Harvey, D. (2006) *Spaces of global capitalism*, London: Verso.

Harvey, D. (2007) *A brief history of neo-liberalism*, Oxford: Oxford University Press.

Harvey, D. (2008) 'The right to the city', *New Left Review*, 53(September–October). Available at https://newleftreview.org/II/53/david-harvey-the-right-to-the-city

Haywood, A. (2011) *End of the affair*, London: Smith Institute.

Healey, J. and Perry, J. (2015) *The overwhelming case for new public housing*, London: Fabian Society.

Hetherington, P. (2015) *Whose land is our land?*, Bristol: Policy Press.

Highbury Group on Housing Delivery (2011) 'Response to consultation on draft NPPF'. Available at: https://www.westminster.ac.uk/file/19281/download?token=tdzWa5v7

Highbury Group on Housing Delivery (2015) 'Highbury Group pre-election statement on housing supply'. Available at: https://www.westminster.ac.uk/highbury-group-documents

Hill, S. (2015) *Reconnecting the citizen and state through community land trusts and land reform*. Available at http://www.wcmt.org.uk/sites/default/files/report-documents/Hill%20S%20Report%202014%20Final.pdf

HM Treasury (2011) The Plan for Growth, London: HMSO.

House of Lords (2016) *Building more homes*, Select Committee on Economic Affairs, April, London: House of Lords. Available at: http://www.publications.parliament.uk/pa/ld201617/ldselect/ldeconaf/20/2002.htm

Hull, A. (2012) *Together at home: A new strategy for housing*, London: IPPR.

IPPR (Institute for Public Policy Research) (2015) *City villages: More homes; better communities,* London: IPPR.

Islington (2015) 'Preventing wasted housing supply supplementary planning guidance'. Available at: https://www.islington.gov.uk/planning/planningpol/pol_supplement/prevent-wasted-housing

JRF (Joseph Rowntree Foundation) (2016) 'Understanding the likely poverty impacts of the extension of Right to Buy to housing association tenants'. Available at: https://www.jrf.org.uk/report/understanding-likely-poverty-impacts-extension-right-buy-housing-association-tenants

Labour Housing Group (1984) *Right to a home,* Nottingham: Spokesman.

Labour Housing Group (2013) *One nation housing policy. Fifty policies for Labour,* London: Labour Housing Group.

Labour Party (2014) *Mobilising across the nation to build the homes our children need,* report of the Lyons Housing Review, London: Labour Party.

Lapavitsas, C. (2013) *Profiting without producing: How finance exploits us all,* London: Verso.

Lefevre, H. (1985) 'Right to the city', in Kofman, E. and Labas, E. (eds) *Writings on cities,* Oxford: OUP.

Lefevre, H. (1991) *The production of space,* Oxford: Wiley/Blackwell.

Lewis, B. (2015) Housing and Planning Bill. Public Bill Committee. 14th hearing. 8 December. Column 584.

Linklater, A. (2015) *Owning the earth,* London: Bloomsbury.

Litchfield, N. and Darin-Drabkin, H. (1980) *Land policy in planning,* London: Hutchinson.

LGA (Local Government Association) (2014) 'Municipal Bonds Agency: revised business case summary'. Available at: http://www.local.gov.uk/documents/10180/11531/MBA+Business+Case+Summary+Mar+14+v3+cover+sheet.pdf/3acfbec9-b33d-46b6-8f27-422ba4658d71

Local Government Association (LGA) (2016) 'Statement', reported in *The Guardian*. Available at: https://www.theguardian.com/money/2016/feb/16/government-discounted-starter-home-plan-buyers

London Assembly (2012) 'Review of mayoral planning decisions'. Available at: http://www.london.gov.uk/moderngov/mgConvert2PDF.aspx?ID=8757

London Labour Housing Group (2015) *Housing policies for London* London: Labour Housing Group.

Lyons, M. (2004) *Placeshaping: A shared ambition for the future of local government,* London: HMSO.

Malpass, P. (2003) 'The wobbly pillar? Housing and the British post-war welfare state', *Journal of Social Policy*, 32(4): 589–606.

Marcuse, P. and Madden, D. (2016) *In defence of housing*, London: VERSO.

Massey, D. and Catalano, A. (1978) *Capital and land*, London: Hodder and Stoughton.

Masterman, C. (ed) (1902) *The heart of the Empire*, London: Fisher Unwin.

Masterman, C. (1907) *To colonise England*, London: Fisher Unwin.

Mayor of London (2012) *Barriers to housing delivery,* London: GLA.

Mayor of London (2014a) *Strategic housing market assessment,* London: GLA.

Mayor of London (2014b) *Barriers to housing delivery – Update,* London: GLA.

Mayor of London (2016) *London Plan Annual Monitoring Report 12 2014/5,* London: GLA.

Merrett, S. (1979) *State housing in Britain*, London: Routledge and Kegan Paul.

Meyer, M. (2009) 'The right to the city in the context of shifting mottos within urban social movements', *CITY*, 12(2/3): 362-374.

Murie, A. (2016) *The right to buy?*, Bristol: The Policy Press.

New London Architecture and GL Hearn (2016) 'London tall buildings survey 2016'. Available at: http://www.newlondonarchitecture.org/docs/1_nla_ir_tall_buildings_single-1.pdf

ODPM (Office of the Deputy Prime Minister) (2003) *Sustainable communities plan*, London: HMSO.

ODPM (2009) *Planning policy statement 1: Eco town supplement*, London: HMSO.

ONS (Office of National Statistics) (2015) 'People population community'.

Payne, S. (2016) 'Examining housebuilder behaviour in a recovering housing market', British Academy, January.

Pearce, T. (2016) 'Speech at Labour Party Conference', 25 September. Available at: http://press.labour.org.uk/post/150909659804/we-are-facing-the-biggest-housing-crisis-in-a

Pugalis, L. and Townsend, A.R. (2013) 'The emergence of "new" spatial coalitions in the pursuit of functional regions of governance', *Regional Science Policy & Practice*, 6(1): 49-67.

Ratcliffe, J. (1976) *Land policy*, London: Hutchinson.

Resolution Foundation (2016) 'Home ownership struggle reaches Coronation Street'. Available at: http://www.resolutionfoundation.org/media/blog/home-ownership-struggle-reaches-coronation-street/

Resolution Foundation and SHELTER (2012) *Housing in transition*, London: Resolution Foundation.

Royal Institute of British Architects (RIBA)(2015) *Homewise report*. Available at: https://www.architecture.com/RIBA/Campaigns%20and%20issues/Assets/Files/HomewiseReport2015.pdf

Royal Institute of Chartered Surveyors (RICS (2012) *Financial viability in planning*, London: RICS. Available at: http://www.rics.org/Documents/Financial%20viability%20in%20planning.pdf

RICS (2016) *Rural land market survey 2016*, London: RICS.

Rolnik, R. (2014) 'Report of UN special rapporteur on housing on visit to UK'. Available at: http://www.ohchr.org/EN/Issues/Housing/Pages/CountryVisits.aspx

Ryan-Collins, J., Lloyd, T. and Macfarlane, L. (forthcoming) *They're not making it anymore: Rethinking economics as if land mattered.*

Rydin, Y. (1986) *Housing land policy*, Aldershot: Gower.

Savills (2013) 'UK residential development land'. Available at: http://pdf.euro.savills.co.uk/residential---other/land-mim-aug13-lr.pdf

SHELTER (2012) *Bricks or benefits? Rebalancing housing investment*, May, London: SHELTER.

SHELTER (2015) 'Statement on starter homes by SHELTER chief executive'. Available at: http://www.mortgagesolutions.co.uk/news/2015/10/07/starter-homes-will-not-solve-affordability-crisis-shelter/

Soja, E. (2011) *Seeking spatial justice*, Minneapolis, MN: University of Minesotta Press.

TCPA (Town and Country Planning Association) (2012) *Creating garden cities and suburbs today*, London: TCPA.

Toulmin Smith, J. (1849) *Government by commissions illegal and pernicious*, London: Edward Stafford.

Transparency International (2015) 'Corruption on your doorstep'. Available at: http://www.transparency.org.uk/publications/corruption-on-your-doorstep/

Whitehead, C. and Williams, P. (2015) *Financing affordable housing in the UK. Building on success?* London: London School of Economics.

INDEX

A

Adonis, A., *City villages* report 47
affordability gap 77
affordability ratios 87, 88
affordable housing 85–91
  deficit 63, 139–41
  definition of 140
  funding 53, 117
  and housing deficit 77–8
  geographical variation 87
  and grants 117
  reduction of 31
  redefinition of 14, 15, 16, 73, 86
  as 'sub-market' 85
  subsidies 139, 140
  and tenure 89
Affordable Housing
  Programme 15t
'affordable rent' programme 13, 14,
  16, 33, 70, 86–8
agricultural land values 69
ALMOs (arm's-length management
  organisations) 29
alternative providers 11, 23
'austerity' politics 31, 32, 33, 124

B

bail outs, banks and building
  societies 30
Balls, Ed 44
Bank of England 37
Barker, Kate 41, 57, 112

Barker review 2004 29, 30, 41, 64
Barwell, Gavin 47
base bank rate 58
'bedroom tax' ('spare room
  subsidy') 101, 102, 103, 107
Benn, Hilary 41
Best, Lord 8
big society 108, 109
Blackman-Woods, Roberta 41
Blair, Tony 37, 51
BNG (Nederlendse
  Gemeenten) 159
Brexit 47, 48
Brown, George 28
Brown, Gordon 37
brownfield sites 44, 76, 115
'Building Britain's future' 58
build-out rates 77, 78
built form 75, 95, 167
Burnley 87
'buy to let' programme 33, 56

C

Cadbury, Ruth 48
Cameron, David 14
capital, financialisation of 26
capital costs funding 29, 53, 54, 69,
  163
capital gains tax 65, 124, 161
capital grants 33, 143
capital investment 15t
capital subsidies 139, 140
centralisation 110

centralism 42, 135
Chartered Institute of Housing 9, 40
Christian communism 27
CIL (Community Infrastructure Levy) 10, 15, 44, 57, 73, 114, 142, 160
CLASS (Centre for Labour and Social Studies) 46
Clegg, Nick 47
Coalition government
affordable homes 31
Community Infrastructure Levy (CIL) 73
county–district structure 131, 132
and development capital 77
financial deregulation 33–5
garden cities initiative 146, 147
and localism 133
London housing 43
Plan for growth 112
planning reform 105–18
policy shift 12, 13–14
and regionalism 149
and social housing 70
Communities Plan 2003 34
Community Infrastructure Levy *see* CIL
commuting 39, 132
compact city concept 74
COMPASS 38, 108
compulsory purchase 22, 116, 143, 144, 153, 154–5
Compulsory Purchase Orders *see* CPOs
Conservative Party
under Cameron 32, 55
consensus with Labour 25
Control shift: Returning power to local communities 109
election manifesto 44–5
Housing Act 1980 7
Housing and Planning Act 2016 7–24
and land value capture system 28
under May 32

national housing output target 55
Open source planning 133
post war 28
and regional planning system 34
and Right to Buy 46
support for homeownership 71
under Thatcher 28
Cooper, Yvette 41
Copeland, Cumbria 87
Corbyn, Jeremy 47, 48
corporate investments 65
Council for the Protection of Rural England (CPRE) 112
council housing *see* local authority housing
council tax 41, 103, 161, 162
CPOs (Compulsory Purchase Orders) 117, 154, 155, 156
CPRE *see* Council for the Protection of Rural England
credit crunch 2008 37, 55, 58, 64

D

decent homes programme 29
Defend Council Housing, 'Kill the Bill' campaign 9
democratic accountability 134
demolition of houses 55
deposits 30, 39, 52, 88
development density 93–5
development viability 106, 113, 114–18, 156–7, 158
direct development 59
direct public sector grants 53
direct public subsidy 78
disposal covenants 103
distribution of housing 26
'distributionalism' 99
Dorling, Danny 26, 103, 160
All that is solid 99
downsizing 103

E

Ebbsfleet 144
eco-towns 14, 74, 75, 76, 132, 143

Edwards, Michael 68
efficiency in housing use 103
emergency housing programme 27
employment
 and housing benefit 33, 56
 and localism 105
 mixed housing 36
 and new development 75–6, 132,
  149–52, 163, 164
 and social housing 38, 39, 128
 and stability 21, 129
 and transport 82
energy standards 142
English Partnerships 58
'English votes for English laws'
 procedure 8, 48
environmental sustainability 112
European Union (EU)
 referendum 1
Examinations in Public 16
Existing Use Value (EUV) 116
ex-service personnel 17

F

Fabian Society 40, 46
Farron, Tim 47
finance for house building 65,
 66–8, 158–9
financial deregulation 30, 33–5
Financial Services Authority 37
Foresight report 2015 68

G

garden cities 9, 74, 75, 76, 146, 147
garden suburbs 74, 79
Geddes, Patrick 12
'Geddes axe' 1922 32
generational affordability 90
global financial crisis 30, 37
'good society' 108
government grants 71, 72, 122, 144,
 158, 163
governance 26–7, 32, 80–1, 108,
 110, 125, 134, 136
grant, average per dwelling 15t

Greater London Authority 81
Greater London Authority Act
 1999 131
Greater Manchester 108
green belt 26, 81, 93, 94, 112
'greenfield land' 94
Growth and Infrastructure Act
 2013 31
growth areas programme 14, 34, 55,
 56, 59, 105, 132

H

HCA (Homes and Communities
 Agency) 13, 58, 70, 86, 116,
 143–6
Healey, Denis 28
Healey, John 46, 48
Help to Buy 39, 44
Hetherington, Peter, *Whose land is
 our land?* 68
Highbury Group on Housing
 Delivery 45, 46
high-rise development 95, 96
homeownership
 and 'buy to let' 33
 and citizenship 36, 37, 51
 desirability of 36–7, 123
 and household wealth 85
 initiatives 29
 and New Labour 51–3
 rising levels of 38
Homes and Communities Agency
 see HCA
House of Commons, Housing and
 Planning Act 2016 8
House of Commons Public Bill
 Committee 8
House of Lords 8
house prices
 and affordable housing 85–8, 139
 'buy to let' and 33
 and economic factors 55, 57, 64
 London 39, 40
 Pathfinders programme and 55
 starter homes and 15

and supply 123, 159
Housing Act 1980 7, 28
Housing Act 1984 53
Housing and Planning Act
   2016 7–24
 flexible tenancies 21
 higher value council homes 18–19
 'pay to stay' 19, 20
 'in principle' planning consent 21,
   22, 23
 Right to Buy 17–18
 starter homes 15–17, 73
 weakening of local authority
   power 22
Housing and Regeneration Act
   2008 143, 157
housing associations
 'affordable rent' 33
 capital grants 29
 cross-subsidy 29
 finance 54
 grants 69, 70, 71
 London 63
 mixed funding regime 69, 70–1
 'pay to stay' 19
 rent increases 34, 88
 'Right to Buy' 10, 44, 17–18
 role of 28
 security 39
housing benefit 13, 33, 106, 107,
   122
Housing Corporation
 affordable housing 54
 HCA and 58, 70
 home ownership 52
 and housing associations 71
 'kickstart' programme 30
 mixed-finance 124
 new-build funding 29
 social housing 13, 28
housing deficit 63–83
 Community Infrastructure Levy
   (CIL) 73
 economic factors 64, 65
 finance of development 65–8
 infrastructure 76, 77–8

 land cost 68, 69
 new development 74–6
 planning 71, 72, 73
 political factors 65
 subsidy 69, 70–1
 sustainable communities 79–83
Housing Individual Savings
   Account (ISA) 44
Housing Revenue Account
   (HRA) 59
housing stock, use of 99–103
Howard, Ebenezer 78

I

IMF (International Monetary
   Fund) 28
'in principle' planning consent 21,
   22, 23
infill suburban development 82
infrastructure 15, 29, 76, 77–8, 81,
   82, 149, 150
inheritance tax 65, 103, 161
international investors 65, 68
investment grants 13
investment subsidies 121, 122, 168
IPPR (Institute for Public Policy
   Research) 37, 40
   Together at Home 122

J

Johnson, Boris 70, 81, 86
joint venture partnerships 76
Jones, C., Coombes, M. and Wong,
   C. 151
Joseph Rowntree Foundation 18
'just city' 27

K

Kelly, Gavin 40
Kerslake, Lord 8
key workers programme 29, 52
Keynesian economics 32, 57
Khan, Sadiq 81
'kickstart' programme 30, 58

L

Labour Housing Group 45
Right to a home 27
Labour Party
  under Attlee 38
  under Blair 28–9, 32, 37, 54
  under Brown 29, 30, 31, 32, 37,
    52–3, 54, 55, 58
  under Callaghan 28, 32
  consensus with Conservatives 25,
    39
  election defeats 39
  election manifesto 43, 44–6
  Finance and Industry Group 45
  and homeownership 37, 40
  and inflation 55
  and Lyons report 42
  'mansion tax' 43
  neoliberalism 28–9
  opposition to Bill 2016 8, 9
  post election 2015 48
  post war 32
  on 'right to buy' 37
  selection of new leader 46, 47, 48
  targets 159
  taxation policy 32
land
  assembly 22, 23, 42
  availability of 78
  cost of 68, 69, 153, 154, 155
  development 154, 155, 167
  land-banking 66
  taxation 69, 159, 160–2
  value capture system 28
Land Registry 69
Lapavitsas, Costas 26
Laying the foundations 35
Lefevre, Henri 26
LEPs *see* local enterprise
  partnerships
Lewis, Brandon 22, 47
Liberal Democrats 8, 43, 47
Linklater, Andro 69
Liverpool 108
Livingstone, Ken 86

local authority housing
  collaborative planning 148
  estate-based reinvestment 53
  'fixed-term tenancies' 11
  forced sale 18–19, 28
  in London 63
  non-renewal of tenancies 18, 21
  'pay to stay' 11, 19, 20
  post war investment 27
  rent increases 29, 88
  residualisation of 20
  see also Right to Buy
local enterprise partnerships
  (LEPs) 107, 108, 148
Local Government Association 8,
  9, 159
local planning authorities *see* LPAs
localism 14, 41, 105, 108–12,
  125–6, 133–8
Localism Act 2011 11, 13–14, 21,
  33, 34, 83, 106–12, 136, 147, 149,
  152
London
  affordability ratios 87–8
  affordable homes 87, 89
  debate re housing 42, 43
  density of housing 93, 94–5
  effective use of housing 102
  Help to Buy 39, 40
  Homes and Communities
    Agency 70
  house prices 39, 40
  housing deficit 63, 126
  international investors 68
  land costs 69, 153
  Mayoral Development
    Corporation (MDC) 144, 145
  planning obligations (section 106
    agreements) 72
  and private rented sector 122
  regional planning structure 105,
    106, 131
  size of new homes 95
  and strategic planning 35, 132
  and sustainable development 81–3
London, Mayor of

affordable rented programme 14,
70, 86
compulsory purchase power 144
election of 45, 47
estate regeneration schemes 58
funding power of 143, 145
'mansion tax' 43
planning powers 35, 147
research on planning consents 67
London Plan 16, 72, 86, 87, 94,
114, 115
LPAs (local planning
authorities) 16, 23, 31, 160, 161,
167
Lyons, Sir Michael 40, 41
Lyons report 2014 41, 42, 151, 153,
154

M

Malpass, P. 34
'mansion tax' 43, 47
market failure 37–8
market rents 19, 20
May, Theresa 47
Miliband, Ed 37, 40, 41, 44, 46
mixed-use allocations 116, 117
mortgages 30, 52, 53, 56, 58, 87
multi-family households 90, 91
Municipal Bonds Agency 159
municipal investment
corporations 159
Murie, A. 141

N

National Housing and Planning
Advisory Unit 151
national planning framework, need
for 130
National Planning Policy Framework
see NPPF
'National planning policy guidance'
(NPPG) 15, 107
national spatial plans 42, 126, 130,
149–51
National Trust 112

Nederlendse Gemeenten
(BNG) 159
Neighbourhood Development
Order 136
neighbourhood planning 134–7,
152–3
neoliberalism 225, 26, 8, 51, 55,
56, 57
new development, location
of 74–6, 97
New Economics Foundation 69
new homes
bonus for 76
funding of 29
requirement for 63
size of 95–6
sustainability of 77
New Labour 13, 51, 54, 108, 110,
132
New Liberals 32
new organisations 144, 145–7
new towns 28
NIMBYs ('not in my
backyard') 111
norm rate of return 156
North East England 90
Northern Ireland 88, 149
Northern Rock 37
NPPF (National Planning Policy
Framework) 14, 15, 16, 78, 86, 106,
107, 112–15, 156
'nudge' theory 111

O

Office for National Statistics
(ONS) 90
off-plan sales 68
Olympic Delivery Agency 145
One Nation Toryism 47, 48
Osborne, George 13
overcrowding 90, 100, 101, 101t

P

pathfinders programme 55
'pay to stay' 11, 19, 20

Pearce, Teresa 48
'permission in principle' 11
Perry, John 46
Pickles, Eric 13
Planning and Compulsory Purchase
    Act 2004 108, 131, 148
'Planning for growth' 14, 112–13
Planning Officer Society 40
planning system 105–18, 137–8,
    139, 147, 148–53
 changes under Coalition 14
 consents 54, 55, 67
 as constraint on supply 64
 gain agreements 29
 local 157
 ministerial power 11, 12
 'permission in principle' 11
 planning obligations (section 106
    agreements) 15, 71, 72, 142
 presumption in favour of
    development 106
 and strategic housing market
    assessment 22
 viability appraisals 42
Policy Exchange 25
Porter, Lord Gary 9
post-war consensus 12, 27
prefabricated houses 27
private developers 28, 29, 142
private rented sector
 deregulation of 122
 housing caps 13
 housing management orders 123
 and lower-income families 18
 rent increases 89
 tenancies 43
public sector organisations and land
    ownership 155
public sector stock renewal
    programmes 53
Public Sector Works Loan
    Board 158

R

rate of return 65
recapitalisation of banks 58
recession 2008 31, 37, 39, 57, 64,
    67, 69
redistribution of housing stock 27
regional planning structure 14, 81,
    107, 149–50
Regional Spatial Strategies
    (RSSs) 131, 133, 134
regional targets, abolition of 14
'registered providers' 29
rent target system 54
rental sector, social and private,
    importance of 77
Resolution Foundation 40, 89–90
retirement housing 17
revenue subsidies 121, 122, 139,
    140
'right to a home' 26, 27
Right to Buy
 encouragement 14
 extension of 10, 44
 housing associations 17–18
 Labour government and 29
 and non-renewal of tenancy 21
 popularity of 51
 proposed abolition of 141
 sale of better houses 39
'right to grow' 148
'right to the city' 26, 27
Royal Institute of Chartered
    Surveyors (RICS) 116
Royal Town Planning Institute
    (RTPI) 9, 134

S

Savills report 2013 66
Scotland 88, 141, 149
second homes 100, 101, 161
secretary of state, power of 12, 23
section 106 agreements 15, 71, 72,
    142
security of tenure, impact of loss
    of 21

Shapps, Grant 76
shared accommodation rate 13
shared ownership programme 13, 29, 52, 70, 87
SHELTER, *Bricks or benefits?* 121, 122
SHOUT (Social Housing Under Threat) 46
Smith Institute (Haywood), *End of the affair: The implications of declining home ownership* 38
Social Democrat Party 109
social housing
government subsidy and 13, 33, 69, 70–1, 106
positive functions of 38, 39–49
residualisation of 7, 35, 36
retention of 141
scapegoating of 35–6
and security 39
spatial concentration of 19, 36
social infrastructure 76, 77–8
compulsory purchase orders and 154
funding for 29, 55, 67, 117, 159, 167
growth and 81–2
organisations 147
responsibility for 131, 150–1, 158
sustainability 79
see also CIL (Community Infrastructure Levy)
soundness test 16
'spare room subsidy' *see* 'bedroom tax'
spatial justice 125–6
'squeezed middle' 40
stamp duty 39, 58, 103, 161
starter homes initiative 10, 11, 12, 15–17, 44, 71, 73
stigmatisation 39
strategic planning 15, 35, 126–30, 141, 142, 143
sub-market housing 13, 14, 29, 87
sub-prime lending 30

sub-regional planning 107, 108, 151, 152
supported housing 71
'survey before plan' 12
sustainable communities 14, 79–83, 105
'sustainable development' 9, 113
sustainable residential quality (SRQ) 94

T

target rent system 29
targets 113, 114–18
taxation
capital gains tax 65, 124, 161
developable sites 42
and efficiency 103
impact of 65
inheritance tax 65, 103, 161
land tax 69, 159, 160–2
for public investment 31, 32
TCPA (Town and Country Planning Association) 9, 40
report 2012 74
tenure conditions 160
Thames Gateway 132
Thatcher, Margaret 51
Toulmin Smith, Joshua 109
Town and Country Planning Act 1947 7, 12, 27, 28
Town and Country Planning Act 1990 71
Transparency International, *Corruption on your doorstep* 68
transport, and planning 19, 67, 72, 73, 75–6, 79, 81–2, 132
'triple lock' 45
trustification of assets 78

U

underbounded authorities 42
under-occupation 100, 101t, 102, 103, 107
UNITE trade union 46

urban extensions 76, 82
US (United States) 30

V

vacant homes 18–19, 100, 101, 129
value maximisation 65, 66
value-capture regime 160
value uplift 154, 155
viability appraisals, accountability
  of 157

W

Wales 149, 141
welfare benefit cap 14, 45
welfare state, as safety net 34

Y

young adults living with parents 90,
  91

Z

zoning 69, 117, 144, 146, 154, 155